Tennessee County History Series

Davidson County

by Frank Burns

Robert B. Jones
Editor

Some days are golden, others lead —
I hope this reminds you only of the gold!
For thirty years of friendship and
in appreciation of all you have done
for me & for the news profession,
here _at last_ is "the book."

April 16, 1989   Frank Burns

MEMPHIS STATE UNIVERSITY PRESS
Memphis, Tennessee

Map prepared by MSU Cartographic Services Laboratory

Manufactured in the United States of America

Designed by Gary G. Gore

ISBN 0-87870-130-3

To Harry Phillips
Writer, Lawyer, Jurist, Counselor

Acknowledgments

To Johnnie, my wife, for her encouragement, and for her professionally competent copyreading of the manuscript.

To my parents, whose memories of Nashville of 1917–1920 inform this portrait of a place and its people.

To the writers and scholars who have gone before along this path and whose trail I have followed using their printed words as a guide.

To the people of Davidson County whose daily lives across the years make up the fabric of this story.

Thank you.

Frank Burns

July 15, 1986

Preface

This is a story of a place. It is a story that has been told before, and told well, by many storytellers. Davidson County as the site of the capital of the state has been the scene of momentous events. Consequently historians have been attracted to the county as a subject for books, both general histories and specialized studies. Moreover the Tennessee County History Series is limited in length; because it is intended for a general audience too much documentation of sources is avoided. The format is that of the personal essay, a narrative flow that draws the reader on by emphasizing cause and effect. My goal has been to select certain incidents from the story of Davidson County that have somehow been overlooked or sketchily treated by other writers and to develop these thoroughly. In this approach the guide has been J. E. Scates, the Memphis educator.

In his book, *A School History of Tennessee* (Memphis, 1925), Scates said that "the concise is the opposite of the elementary. Instead of the usual hurried summary a concise history should select the most important persons, events, and movements and tell of them with some richness of detail." This is the method I have followed, realizing that many persons of note have been omitted or mentioned by name only in passing; that events have been passed over; and that movements important to contemporary residents of Davidson County have assumed lesser importance in the perspective of later developments (the crucial question of public debt which marked the 1880s, the temperance issue which burned so hotly from 1899 to 1939, the battle for woman's suffrage, which divided friend from friend up to 1919, for example). Because Nashville is the capital of the state there have been many events of statewide importance. I have chosen to ignore most of these which did not also have particular significance to the county even if the legislative battles did happen to occur within the county boundaries or the administrative decisions happened to be made by a chief executive whose home was temporarily within the city. Thus, while the formation of the metropolitan government is treated in some detail, the campaign for secession is not. The ratification of the nineteenth amendment in Nashville was most important to the state and nation, but even if the leaders of women on both sides were of Nashville and Davidson County this is not treated as an event of county history.

Having some experience with scholarly writing in my own academic field, I am aware of the demands of that form; recognizing the validity of George Orwell's strictures in his essay on style, "Politics and the English Language," I am not averse to writing prose that is acceptable to the general public. Accuracy of idea has been my aim; I trust there are no inaccuracies of fact. Trustworthiness is the fundamental requirement for history.

G. Frank Burns

*D*AVIDSON COUNTY was organized in 1783, Fort Nashborough having been established by the James Robertson party on December 25, 1779. The county is 508 square miles in area and is located on both sides of the Cumberland River. From the north clockwise it is bounded by Robertson, Sumner, Wilson, Rutherford, Williamson, and Cheatham counties. Generally the land is gently rolling although there are hills of considerable height on all sides of the county seat, Nashville, forming three long ridges: Paradise Ridge, part of the Highland Rim, northwest of Nashville from which Marrowbone, White's, and Mansker's creeks descend; Harpeth Ridge, the watershed between the Cumberland and Harpeth Rivers; and a ridge which divides the Harpeth from the Little Harpeth River. The soil of Davidson County is mostly fertile, except for the rocky area of the Marrowbone Hills in the northwest; there are surface rocks in almost every part of the county and limestone strata are nowhere very far below the surface. This has been a problem to contractors working with water and sewer lines but has provided a firm foundation for the tall buildings of the city skyline. Most of this stone is an outcrop of the Nashville and Cincinnati formations. The rock to build the State Capitol was excavated from a fairly deep bed of limestone in the state quarry, once located west of

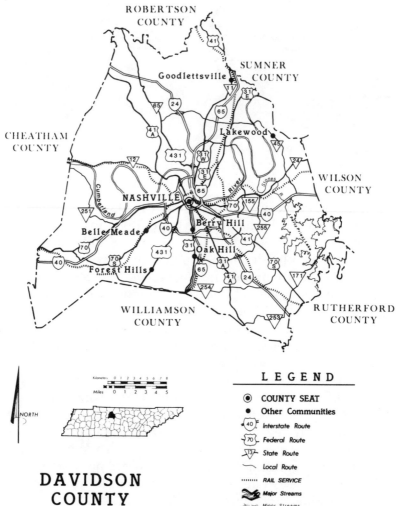

ROBERTSON
COUNTY

SUMNER
COUNTY

Goodlettsville

CHEATHAM
COUNTY

Lakewood

WILSON
COUNTY

NASHVILLE

Berry Hill

Belle Meade

Oak Hill

Forest Hills

WILLIAMSON
COUNTY

RUTHERFORD
COUNTY

NORTH

DAVIDSON
COUNTY

MSU Cartographic Services Laboratory

L E G E N D

⦿ COUNTY SEAT
● Other Communities
🛡40 Interstate Route
〔70〕 Federal Route
〈13〉 State Route
⌄ Local Route
········· RAIL SERVICE
〰 Major Streams
⤳ Minor Streams

SOURCE: Tennessee Department of Transportation

the building. Resembling sandstone, it is actually limestone, laminated, bluish gray with dark bands. The bed underlies most of the city and some of this stone was also quarried at the foot of Gay Street on the river. Another type of native stone which was used for the fronts of many of Nashville's distinguished buildings of the mid-nineteenth century was called Bosley stone.

In 1980 the population of Davidson County was 477,811; in 1970 it was 447,877; in 1960, 399,743. Incorporated towns in 1980 were Belle Meade (population 3182); Berry Hill (1113); Forest Hills (4516); Goodlettsville (8327); Lakewood (2325); Nashville (455,651); Oak Hill (4609); and Ridgetop (1225). The municipalities of Goodlettsville and Ridgetop are shared with Sumner and Robertson counties respectively. Nashville has been chartered since 1962 as the Metropolitan Government of Nashville and Davidson County; there are two districts: the Urban Services District and the General Services District. The U.S. Department of Commerce has only the former in its report of urban population.

Davidson County was named in honor of General William Lee Davidson, the "Piedmont Partisan." This distinguished North Carolinian was born in Lancaster County, Pennsylvania, in 1746, the family removing to the Catawba Valley of North Carolina in 1748. With the approach of the American Revolution he was appointed one of the twenty-five members of Rowan County's Committee of Correspondence. North Carolina authorized the formation of two regiments to be a part of the Continental Army, as distinguished from the Minute Men. In mid-April of 1776 these regiments were expanded to six, and Davidson was appointed major of the Fourth North Carolina, under Colonel Thomas Polk. After participating in several actions in the South, the regiment joined General George Washington and the Continental Line in Pennsylvania in the fall of 1777, fighting in the Battle of Germantown. Among the dead was Francis Nash, commanding general of the North Carolina troops and the man for whom Fort Nashborough (and therefore Nashville) was named two years later. Davidson served with Washington's army at Valley Forge and was ordered with his troops to return south in the spring of 1778. By then a lieutenant colonel, he went south, but in December returned to Washington's command and was stationed at West Point. Washington was convinced that the war would be won in the South. Therefore he ordered Davidson to rejoin his regiment at Charleston in January of 1780. From that time on, the war in the Piedmont region of the Carolinas grew more and more fierce; the contending armies were in constant action. On February 1, 1781, defending a crossing of the Catawba River at Cowan's Ford against the soldiers of Lord Cornwallis, William Davidson, brigadier general commanding, was killed. His troops had for crucial months held western North Carolina for the cause of independence. Ten months later at Yorktown Cornwallis surrendered. It is recorded that half a century later old men wept when they told the story of Davidson's death. Many of his soldiers were among those who built the settlement on the Cumberland that bears his name.

The Role the French Played

They called the river Chauvanons—River of the Shawnees. They were the French traders, coming down from Vincennes; the same traders and soldiers of the King of France who claimed the sovereignty of the Mississippi Valley west of the mountains, who established a fort called Prudhomme on the bluffs of the Chickasaw Nation above the great river Mississippi. The large stream flowing into the Ohio a little way below the river of the Shawnees they called the Tcheraquis (Tennessee), the river of the Cherokees. It had been a forest land full of game, a rich land, first the Iroquois, then the Shawnee claiming jurisdiction. A great war had been fought between the Shawnee and the Cherokee, who were victorious. It was a great power war like those being waged at the same time in Europe, for reasons, it must be said, far less vital to national interests. But it was a war that would have incalculable results as the Europeans in America extended their system of alliances into a new world already divided into rival powers and sophisticated strategies: the Iroquois and their kin were wooed by the French, the Cherokee by the English, the Creek by the Spanish. Each Indian nation chose a European power, each for its own reason having nothing to do with European politics but having a great deal to do with native American politics, a politics little or not at all understood by the European.

But now the bluffs of the River Chauvanons (Cumberland) were in a hunting preserve patrolled by Cherokees. Here the French built a stockade and cabins to house themselves and their trading goods, not as a permanent settlement, because the French did not think in those terms, but as a place near a great salt lick which attracted the animals that the Cherokee hunting parties sought, and therefore would be convenient to Cherokee purchasers of trade goods. And later, after the Peace of 1763 had decided that the country between the Mississippi and the mountains would not be French but English—or at least under the sovereignty of King George III who in his wisdom then forbade his American subjects from crossing those mountains to make permanent settlements although allowing them to trade with his Redskin friends—the French abandoned that trading post, called French Lick, except for Timothy deMonbrun, who continued to ply his vocation of storekeeper. (His proper name was Jacques Timothe Boucher, Sieur de Mont Brun. He had moved to the French Lick in the 1760s knowing that the bluffs had been a good place for trade, Jean de Charleville's fur trading post having been built there in 1710.)

Mr. Robertson's County

Davidson County has passed through many eras. To each of these the name of some person can be attached: some of heroic stature, some whose characteristics are typical of the age, some whom chance thrust into a position of prominence. The name of James Robertson has acquired the golden laurel of the hero, an Augustus of his time.

Yet he was not the first settler, nor the leader of the first settlers, nor even the first permanent resident of Davidson County. Jacques Timothe Boucher de Montbrun was that: like Robertson's his progeny still are residents. The year of his arrival is set as 1760. And he was not first. He found six white men and one white woman near the river in the present Montgomery County. In the autumn of 1777 de Montbrun went to Vincennes, British headquarters for the Northwest territories, leaving his hunting and trading partner, LeFevre, alone at the French Lick.

The following year (the American Revolution was pitting neighbor against neighbor in the Carolinas) about thirty English-speaking Tory families attempted to colonize the Cumberland; de Montbrun had dealings with them. Apparently they moved on across Kentucky, into Ohio. That winter (1778–79) Robertson and several companions came by canoe to the Lick for the first time and met not only de Montbrun and three other Frenchmen (all were Canadians), but a settler names Jones (Thomas Jones from Pennsylvania?) who had built a cabin and cleared a corn field in Jones' Bend, where the first house of Andrew Jackson was later erected in 1794. Clover Bottom, on Stone's River, had also been cleared and planted in corn before 1780 by Michael Stoner, whose name still survives in the name of Stoner's Creek.

It had been in 1777 at Long Island in East Tennessee that Robertson, John Donelson, and Richard Henderson, there for the signing of the treaty of that name, met and discussed western settlement. Although Robertson wanted to take a party to French Lick in the spring of 1779, having been pleased by the findings of his party that winter, it was the autumn before everything was ready. Among other things Col. George Rogers Clark owned cabin rights in a tract of 3000 acres at the Lick which he had bought from a Virginia militia officer in 1776. Once Clark's cabin rights claims were proven invalid the way was clear for the permanent settlement by Robertson. Two parties were formed: one to go overland through Kentucky, taking horses and other livestock, the second to travel by boat down the Tennessee, up a short stretch of the Ohio, and up the Cumberland to the French Lick. Donelson would command the flotilla, which had many women and children aboard. Robertson on horseback started his march first. John Donelson (1718?–1786), also a native of Virginia and a member of the Commonwealth's House of Burgesses, came with his family to Watauga and met with Robertson and Henderson. His group of settlers bound for the French Lick traveled aboard the flatboats, along the three rivers as planned, arriving in the spring after many dangers, enduring some deaths and illness.

The Donelson family settled on Stone's River but moved to Kentucky has the hostilities with the Indians intensified. In 1786 he decided to return and sent his family south to Mansker's Station in the northeastern part of Davidson County. After a time he started south, encountering two young men along the way. The two companions arrived in Nashborough with a tale that Donelson had been shot and fatally wounded by Indians. How they escaped while the more experienced frontiersman was killed they could not explain but they were cleared of suspicion. The murder remains mysteriously unsolved.

Robertson (1742–1814), a native of Virginia but removed to North Carolina as a child, had gone with several other families to the newly founded Watauga settlements in East Tennessee in 1768, becoming a judge. After the establishment of the Cumberland settlement at French Lick, he was the leading citizen of Nashborough. Indeed on January 15, 1781, the night of his return from a foraging trip to Kentucky, he saved the new colony when he heard the sound of stealthy warriors outside the walls of Freeland's Station, where his wife Charlotte had gone to stay with friends soon after the birth of their son Felix. Sounding the alarm, he took command and fought off the hostile tribesmen. In April a more serious attack was made and what has been called the Battle of the Bluffs ensued. This time the hero was Mrs. Robertson, who turned loose the dogs from the fort and diverted the attention of the enemy long enough for Robertson and his men, cut off by the surpise attack, to regain the walls. James and Charlotte Reeves Robertson (1751–1843) had earned their title, "Saviors of Nashville."

In 1783 North Carolina created Davidson County, technically from that state's Washington County. In 1786 Sumner County was taken from the northern and eastern parts of Davidson; Tennessee County to the north and west was cut off two years later. In 1801 the General Assembly of Tennessee extended Davidson County's boundary south to the state line. Once the Indian claims to the southern lands were cleared, new counties were set up there and the county assumed its present dimensions. (The eastern boundary with Wilson was also adjusted in 1801.)

Davidson County took no part in the establishment of the State of Franklin in 1784. It may have been because the Watauga leadership believed those in Davidson opposed separation from North Carolina that the western boundary of Franklin was set by the enabling act as a line from the Falls of the River Ohio (present Louisville) directly south to Elk River, passing east of Nashville by some fifty miles. It should be noted that in 1796 the vote in Davidson on statehood was 94 for the new state, 517 against.

Communities of Davidson County

In 1960 the U.S. Bureau of Census recognized 32 suburban communities in Davidson County. Bordeaux, Goodlettsville, Haynes Heights, Inglewood, Joelton, Madison, Maplewood, Ridgetop, Scottsboro, are north of Cumberland River. Antioch, Belle Meade, Berry Hill, Crieve Hall, Donelson, Dupontonia, Early, Forest Hills, Glencliff, Glendale, Green Hills, Harpeth, Hermitage, Hillwood, Oak Hill, Old Hickory, Providence, Radnor, Richland, West Meade, Woodbine, Woodmont, are south of the river.

In the early days there were other named communities.

White's Creek Pike goes northwest of Nashville from the Cumberland River to the county line. The land was settle early. Frederick Stump and Amos Heaton and their families reached there in late 1779 and built Heaton's Station the next spring. By 1809 the White's Creek settlement was largely owned by the wealthy and influential Stumps.

Stump set the pattern for country living on White's Creek. When he died in 1822 at the age of 99 he owned 1493 acres. This had been expanded from a land grant of 640 acres close to Buena Vista Ferry (originally Barrow's). Along the creek he built an inn, operated a mill, cultivated fields of corn, and lived in peace with his neighbors and friends.

In 1797 William Nolen came with his family from Virginia to Tennessee in a covered wagon. In the canebrakes south and east of the Cumberland settlement a wheel on the wagon broke. While repairs were being made (and this took a great deal of time) Nolen looked about him, at the beautiful country, good soil and water, and decided to settle there. The community that sprang up was called Nolensville, the road that still goes that way is Nolensville Road. Two notable houses were built along that road: Grassmere, one of the earliest brick residences, and Wrencoe, once the center of a large farm. Grassmere House, built by Michael C. Dunn, who also was a Virginian, has been willed with its 309 acres to the Cumberland Museum and Science Center for nature study by Elise and Margaret Croft, fifth generation descendants of Colonel Dunn. The land will demonstrate farming methods used at each period of Davidson County history.

Wrencoe, today a solid and dignified two-storey white frame structure with a full two-storey columned porch that extends the width of the house, surrounds the original house, one large room above another identical room, with stairway connecting and a fireplace in each. Standing at Mill Creek, the original house was the center of Wrencoe village: post office, dry goods store, blacksmith shops serving the needs of the nearby farmers.

Not far away on Edmondson Pike, stands the John Chambers house, built well before the Civil War by the Turrentine family. Destroyed by fire in 1941 but rebuilt to the same plan that year, the house is a reminder of two names prominent in the community called Tusculum, a neighborhood closely knit by kinship, common interests, and shared traditions.

At the crossing of Mill Creek by the northern fork of the Murfreesboro dirt road stood the fort of Major John Buchanan where an attack by Indians coming up the Black Fox trail was repelled in the early days of the settlement. This road, where Buchanan's Mill was located in 1809, led to the old Jackson & Coffee storehouse at Clover bottom, crossed Stone's River and proceeded to the Hermitage lane before going on to Lebanon.

This was then considered the best land in Davidson County for cotton farming and the best section in which to live. Here where the Donelsons and the Wards, the Overtons, Winstons, and Gleaveses. These were large landowners, with many acres and slaves to work them. On the southern fork of Mill Creek, which led to Murfreesboro, Foster's Mill was located on the water and Sangster's Tavern on the hill beyond.

Between the Franklin Turnpike on the east and the Natchez Trace on the west, near Vaughn's gap, from the county line north to just above Sugar Tree Creek, was the old 11th civil district. Here, on the turnpike from Nashville toward Franklin, lived for many years "Granny" White who kept the only inn and house of entertainment between those two places. She was a friend of Senator Thomas Hart Benton, who lived on the adjoining farm before he removed to Missouri. Indeed Benton referred to her by name in several speeches delivered on the floor of the U.S. Senate.

Her husband, Zachariah White, had come to Nashborough in the earliest days and put in a crop but he was killed in the Battle of the Bluffs. In 1803 Mrs. White and her two orphaned grandchildren came from North Carolina to take up his grant and operate the famous tavern, which was conveniently located for travelers using the Natchez Trace only four miles to the west. After her death in 1815 she was buried near her cabin.

The Cumberland Compact

In 1846 the historian Albigence Waldo Putnam found the original Cumberland Compact in an old trunk which had belonged to Samuel Barton, one of the 256 men who had signed the document and one of the 12 representatives in the Tribunal of Notables, or General Arbitrators, who first governed the infant Cumberland settlements. Written in a fair hand and signed on May 13, 1780, the document as found lacked its first page and was mutilated and defaced on its second, but it is still a remarkable tribute to the faith that Americans have in written law. It is now generally believed that the Compact was the work of Col. Richard Henderson, the patron of the Transylvania Land Company, of which empire the new settlements were considered to be a part.

Settlers who signed the Compact were from eight stations: Fort Union, Donelson's, Bledsoe's, Asher's, Gasper's (Kasper Mansker's), Eaton's, Freeland's, and Nashborough (there was a ninth, Thompson's, that is a shadowy presence in some accounts). The 12 Notables were Samuel Barton, J. J. Blackemore, Isaac Bledsoe, Andrew Ewin, George Freeland, Isaac Lindsey, Thomas Mallory, James Mauldin, James Robertson, David Rounsevall, James Shaw, Ebenezer Titus, and Heydon Wells. Ewin was elected clerk, and presumably Shaw was elected to fill his seat on "The Committee," as the body preferred to call itself in its minutes.

Samuel Barton was born in Virginia in January of 1749, was bound as an apprentice as a youth, took part in Lord Dunmore's War as a ranger in 1774, and during the American Revolution served in the Seventh Virginia Regiment, Morgan's Rifles. Whether he came to Nashborough with James Robertson's party is not known—he may have joined that group somewhere in Kentucky, as did a party from South Carolina—but he told his son Gabriel that he had come "where there were but four families residing in the place." At any rate, Barton was a signer of the Compact and served as one of the Notables. In 1783 a second Compact was drawn up and signed by ten leaders including Barton; in April of that year, when North Carolina established the county of Davidson, he was appointed a justice of the peace. The county court then elected Barton entry taker. He became second major of militia, and a commissioner of the new town of Nashville. When Davidson became a county of the new state of Tennessee in 1796 he was commissioned one of the justices of the peace and colonel of militia. But in 1798, not yet 50 years old, Samuel Barton gave up all of this and moved with his family to what would the next year become Wilson County, to a large plantation on Jennings' Fork of Round Lick Creek. He took up the vocation of surveyor in addition to his extensive farming operations. Undoubtedly one of the reasons Barton left Nashville was the dispute over disposition of the funds of Davidson Academy and the matter of 640 acres of land given the Reverend Thomas Craighead to persuade him to come to Nashville as preacher and teacher at the Academy. On September 4, 1797, Samuel Barton filed a lawsuit against two members of the Academy board, Lardner Clarke and James Robertson. Craighead's daughter had married Robertson's son and the family ties made the issue even more sensitive. Already the matter had cost Barton £640 hard money and threatened to cost him as sole solvent surety up to £900 which he sought to recover from the trustees. The dates of the suit and Barton's removal coincide, so it is reasonable to suppose some connection. In May of 1810 Samuel Barton died.

The Ore Expedition

The Cumberland settlements did not become safe until 1794, although by 1790 almost every acre of Davidson County had been claimed by settlers or holders of land grants. Cabins had been built and land cleared along Harpeth and Marrowbone as well as in all the bends of the river. Some of the land was never settled by the North Carolina soldiers of the America Revolution to whom it had been granted in lieu of back pay. Speculators had bought it up and in turn sold it to land-needy families in the seaboard states or in East Tennessee. These families soon heard that they had better remain east of Cumberland Mountain until the hostility of the Cherokees and the Chickamaugas, stirred up by agents of the British crown during the recent war, had been abated. But the central government offered no help. It was Governor William Blount (of the Territory South of the River Ohio— Tennessee was not yet a state) who offered a tiny force (60 soldiers) under command of Major Ore as guards. Ore went straight to Fort Nashborough. Robertson, commander of militia, completely without authority, mustered 550 mounted men and ordered them to follow the trail of the Chickamauga. They went to the Chickamauga towns of Nickajack and Running Water, in the area of present-day Chattanooga, and destroyed them, ending the danger. A new era was about to begin.

Davidson County in 1795 had a population of 3613. Of these, 728 were free white males, 16 and over, 695 were free white males under 16; 1192 were free white females of all ages; 6 were other free persons (presumably but not necessarily free blacks); and 992 were slaves. It was a largely agricultural society.

Already a Place of Music: The Sacred Harp

The Sacred Harp is a song book, published in 1844, oblong in shape and durable in form, first compiled by two Georgia musicians, Benjamin Franklin White and E. J. King. The songs in the book were, however, composed at a much earlier date and the song that bears the title "Nashville" was attributed to a composed named Alexander Johnson, with words written in 1800 by a well-known singing teacher, Jeremiah Ingalls, who had edited a collection of his own. Because Nashville had since 1800 been a center of religious music, the naming of a tune for the city was logical: there were other tunes named for Southern places— Manchester, Montgomery, Wilson, Carthage, Abbeville, Columbus, Corinth, Jackson—following an old English custom. There is no specific reference to Nashville in the lyrics: "The Lord into his garden come, The spices yield their rich perfumes; The spices yield their rich perfumes, the lilies grow and thrive."

However, Nashville was not and is not a center for Sacred Harp singing, the land farther south from Georgia to Texas being more hospitable, perhaps because of an apparent relationship to the various Baptist bodies rather than to the slightly more formal Methodist and Presbyterian congregations of Davidson County. Buell Cobb, an authority on Sacred Harp singing, conjecturs that carpeted floors were acoustically not suited to the resonances of the unaccompanied vocal music and that it found its true home in one-room country church buildings.

Andrew Jackson's Town

On October 26, 1788, a young lawyer, who had been practicing law in Jonesborough and had already fought one duel there before deciding to pursue his destiny in a new town, arrived in Nashville on the Cumberland. It was not because of the duel— his first—but because opportunity called. Andrew Jackson did not go west alone; there were many other new settlers in the party. With him was John McNairy, friend of the young lawyer and judge of the superior court of the western district of North Carolina, who had appointed him public prosecutor.

Nashville was small, a few hundred inhabitants living in log cabins, some houses, frame or a few of brick, even tent shelters. There were the courthouse, two stores, two taverns, and a distillery. One of the houses was the blockhouse in which John Donelson's widow lived with her family, including a pretty daughter, Rachel, newly separated from her husband. Jackson was accepted as a boarder.

A recent biographer (Robert V. Remini) comments: "No American ever had so powerful an impact on the minds and spirit of his contemporaries as did Andrew Jackson. No other man ever dominated an age spanning so many decades. No one, not Washington, Jefferson, or Franklin, ever held the American people in such near-total submission."

It then was no wonder that from 1795 when the people of Davidson County elected him as delegate to the new state's first constitutional convention, with James Robertson and John McNairy, until 1840 when Whig ascendancy ended his dominance of public life Nashville was Andy Jackson's town.

A Coming Man

Public office came to Jackson swiftly after his first service. Delegate, then unsuccessful candidate for major general of militia, he began his move to power in 1796 with election to the U.S. House of Representatives. William Blount, who had been appointed first (and only) governor of the Territory of the United States South of the River Ohio, was to be one of the two new senators. Blount saw Jackson as a coming man. There were to be three federal offices: he and William Cocke were going to the Senate, Jackson got the third position. When Blount, harassed by threatened impeachment, did not run for reelection, Jackson took his Senate seat, but he resigned in 1798 to accept election as a superior court judge. In 1802 he was elected major general of the Tennessee militia. Meanwhile he had married Rachel, ac-

Rachel and Andrew Jackson's first house on The Hermitage plantation
was a log cabin. (from a post card, about 1905)

quired property on Hunter's Hill, and founded the first Masonic
lodge in Nashville, as well as having become a businessman,
forming a mercantile firm with several branches in nearby
county seat towns. Things were looking up for the Jacksons who
had also acquired land in the eastern part of the county on which
their home, The Hermitage, would be built.

Two other events occurred which might have spoiled the picture: Aaron Burr involved the new major general in his con-
spiracy to take control of the western lands and Jackson killed a
man in a duel: Charles Dickinson. He survived both scandals.

And the county moved on: Davidson Academy was chartered, Congress granted lands to support academies and Cumberland and Blount colleges. The Bank of Nashville was
chartered in 1807; four years later a branch of the Bank of Tennessee opened in Nashville.

Old Hickory's Soldiers

Then the call of war sounded in Davidson County. Jackson, at The Hermitage, knew it was coming and issued a call for volunteers, as major general of militia, in March of 1812: "We are going to fight for the reestablishment of our national character, for the protection of our maritime citizens, to vindicate our right to free trade."

Jackson got his regular army commission as major general. The next 12 months were to make a national hero and a president. With 3000 men he took the Gulf port of Pensacola on November 7, 1814. The defense of New Orleans then became the general's urgent concern. Mobilizing every soldier he could find, he set up the American defenses along the Rodriguez Canal east and north of the city. The British attacked. Although they made command errors, it was the shrewdness of Jackson's troop dispositions, taking advantage of favorable terrain, that won the day. For a generation it was a mark of much pride to point to a man on the streets of Nashville and say: "He was with Jackson at New Orleans."

Andrew Davis, born a slave, found in 1908 that his earliest memories were of the soldiers returning from New Orleans. "I heard them tell their tales of war," he said. "I saw them get off their horses and kiss the ground for joy that they were home again. I saw General Andrew Jackson in his uniform, all blue and shiny buttons." It was an image that filled all Davidson County with pride, would carry "Old Hickory" to the White House, and made Nashville Andy Jackson's town until his death.

A New Decade

The 1820s were busy; in 1819 President Monroe visited; in 1820 The Bank of Tennessee, at Nashville, was incorporated by the General Assembly. In 1823 Jackson, who had been Territorial Governor of Florida, was elected to the U.S. Senate. In 1824 a turnpike from Murfreesboro to Nashville was chartered. La-Fayette visited Nashville in 1825 and the next year Judge John Haywood, called "The Father of Tennessee History" died. And Sam Houston moved into center stage.

Mr. Houston on Trial

A long-forgotten episode in the stormy life of Sam Houston, occurring not long after he moved onto the national scene as a member of the House of Representatives, is to be found in the Proceedings of the Grand Lodge of Tennessee for 1825.

In October of that year Houston, 32 years old and a Congressman, appeared before an evening session of the meeting of the Grand Lodge in Nashville complaining of "slanderous expressions" by Gen. George W. Gibbs. General Gibbs was one of those types so often found in the early public life of Tennessee—a lawyer, a soldier, and a politician. He came to the Calfkiller Valley at an early date, was one of the first lawyers in White County, and had been elected to the state Senate. During the War of 1812 he resigned his Senate seat and went into the army, becoming a general officer.

Houston had heard General Gibbs make a public speech criticizing Major John Eaton, a close friend of both Houston and Senator Andrew Jackson. Houston told Eaton about it. When Gibbs denied making the critical remarks, Houston set to work to prove that the General was not only a slanderer but a liar. Proceeding to interview other persons who had been at the speaking, he took down their statements. Gibbs resented Houston's actions and, the Congressman was told, "had taken the liberty of using certain charges against his veracity and character," to quote the formal language of the Masonic minutes. This was on March 6, 1825, at Murfreesboro. Then Governor William Carroll (Houston believed), no friend of Houston, spread Gibbs' comments all over Nashville. What irked Houston, a man whose temper was easily provoked, was that Carroll repeated the language in front of Wilkins Tannehill, Grand Master of Tennessee Masons, and the Grand Master refused to state in writing what the comments were.

Freemasonry was in those days not only a fraternal order but a real center of political power in the state, a ready-made network of friendships that could offer the young politician quick access to high places. So Congressman Houston was ready to believe that an attempt was being made to discredit him within the circles of the order.

In June Houston was called before a joint meeting of Cumberland Lodge No. 8 and Nashville Lodge No. 37 and resolutions were passed that criticized him. He protested. After long debate the resolutions were withdrawn, but Tannehill again antagonized Houston when he refused to permit consideration of a resolution that supported the Congressman.

"You know that there is a difference between you and Brother Gibbs," he told Houston. "Rumor has it all over town."

"I know that rumor has a thousand tongues, and five hundred are slanderous," Houston retorted.

Tannehill turned away, muttering to the others present: "Let them settle it themselves."

Throughout the summer of 1825 the matter was stirred. Rumors began to be heard, told by persons who were not members of the Masonic order, that Congressman Houston had been censured by the two Nashville lodges. Not only was Houston facing an election for his Congressional seat, but he was already eyeing Carroll's chair as governor. He decided that the whole thing must be settled soon. He petitioned the Grand Lodge to take jurisdiction. That body did so, first passing a resolution intended to soothe the sensibilities of its Grand Master. After all the sound and fury the resolutions that finally were adopted tried to pacify everyone. Houston, the Grand Lodge said, "has acted correctly and honorably throughout the whole transaction," but neither was there reason to censure either Gibbs or Tannehill. Vainly did Tannehill try to point out the inconsistency.

"If one has done right, the other has injured him," he protested. The meeting adjourned.

A Family of Educators

After Davidson Academy became Cumberland College, with Presbyterian leanings, in 1825 Cumberland College became the University of Nashville (the Cumberland Presbyterians had established their Cumberland College at Princeton, Kentucky— later the name would come back to Middle Tennessee). Philip

Lindsley, professor of languages at the College of New Jersey (Princeton), was considering three offers that year. He could become president of the University of Ohio, vice-president of the college at Princeton, or president of the small, struggling college in Tennessee. He chose the latter because of family ties.

During the Revolutionary War his father-in-law, Nathanael Lawrence, a student at the College of New Jersey, was leaning on the fence in front of the Nassau Inn when the North Carolina regiment of the Continental Line came marching past. He joined up for the duration, became a lieutenant and an original member of the Society of the Cincinnati after the war. He was on the Long Room of Fraunces' Tavern in New York City when George Washington bade farewell to his companions in arms of 1783. When North Carolina established its Military Reservation in Tennessee, granting land as past due service pay, Lawrence received two tracts of 2560 acres each. The young officer's daugher married Philip Lindsley. From Nashville Philip could conveniently operate the "Big Survey" on Spring Creek in Wilson County. He accepted the offer from the University of Nashville. (In 1844 he sent a son, Nathanael Lawrence Lindsley, to Cumberland University in Lebanon as professor of languages; five years later the son established Greenwood Seminary on the tract).

President Lindsley put together an outstanding faculty, and before his resignation in 1850 the university had graduated 432 students. The school, and the Nashville Female Academy, founded in 1816 and becoming the largest school for girls in the United States, were among the bright stars of the Jacksonian city.

Billy Carroll

He was born in Pennsylvania in 1788 and came to Nashville in 1810. He soon became one of the leading merchants of the town. At the outbreak of the War of 1812, William Carroll was made major-general of Tennessee militia, when Andrew Jackson was elevated to major-general of the United States Army. He returned from the war a popular figure. He enlarged his business interests and was one of the owners of the first steamboat to come to Nashville wharf. By 1821 Carroll had become interested in politics. He was elected governor in that year, and then was reelected twice. The constitution forbade a fourth consecutive term and he stood aside while Sam Houston took the chair. Would he have been satisfied with the six years of service if Houston had not resigned? At any rate he was a candidate again in 1829, was elected and reelected twice again. Only John Sevier and Carroll have ever been elected governor six times or served twelve full years. A genuine progressive, Carroll had one of the most successful administrations in the history of the state. His campaign promises were carried out: a state prison system; a hospital specifically to treat mental illness; a comprehensive program of river, road, and bridge improvement; reform of the state's tax structure; and finally a new constitution drastically different from that of 1796, particularly in the system of state courts and the organization of county civil districts, replacing the former "captain's companies" of the obsolescent militia organizations. It was in 1822, during Governor Carroll's first term, that the first bridge across the Cumberland River at Nashville was constructed. This was to be known as "the covered bridge." Substantial and elegant in its design, the bridge crossed from the northeast corner of the Public Square to the Gallatin road on the opposite side. The cost was $85,000. However, the elevation was not sufficient for later river traffic and in 1855, 11 years after Carroll's death, it was removed and replaced by the even more famous suspension bridge.

Governor Houston Has Left His Wife!

The most shocking event of the 1820s was the separation of Govenor Houston and his beautiful young wife. This unfortunate romance and marriage and Houston's abrupt termination of it caused him to abandon a promising political career in Tennessee, which might have taken him to the White House.

The ball where Houston in 1828 met Eliza Allen, the young woman who would become his bride, was held in the Brittain Drake house, which stood on the main road several miles east of the Hermitage. Houston, 31 years old, became governor of Ten-

The covered bridge across the Cumberland River at Nashville in 1831. (sketched reproduction of Charles Alexander Lesueur's sketch in the collection of the American Antiquarian Society)

nessee in 1827 and in the summer and fall of 1828 worked hard for the election of Andrew Jackson to the presidency. He and Jackson were invited to attend the ball and so were other prominent politicians. Eliza Allen was a sister of United States Representative Robert Allen of Gallatin. When Houston was serving in the Congress he had been presented to Allen's teenaged sister, but was not impressed. Eliza came to the ball in the company of her Caruthers kin, of Lebanon. Houston saw the young woman with violet eyes and braided blonde hair and was smitten by the 19-year-old beauty as he had not been by the schoolgirl.

The Allens, it is fair to say, recognized that this would be a match that could hold much promise. Houston was not only governor, assured of reelection, a protege of the man who was sure to be president. He was also handsome, ambitious, and likely to be himself some day an aspirant to the presidency. Houston visited John Allen in Gallatin, as he had done before, but this time it was as a suitor. His suit was accepted. The marriage, celebrated at the candlelit Allen home on January 22, 1829, did not last. History was made in its breach. Less than three months later they parted for reasons that are still unknown. But the repercussions sent Houston to Texas in despair. There he met his true destiny. He did indeed become president, but President of the Republic of Texas. Aaron Burr's dream had become Sam Houston's reality.

Why did they part? The newlyweds had not gotten along smoothly from the wedding night, according to friends. Had Houston, as some biographers assert without documentation, had a Cherokee consort during the time the youth spent with the tribe in East Tennessee? And did Houston confess this to a sensitive young bride, not realizing the shock this might be? Or was it that he realized she still cherished a prior attachment to another? Was there a physical incompatibility? At any rate, Sam Houston suffered a broken heart, for a while at least. One of the bridesmaids at the wedding said years later that Eliza told her of a strange incident. The Allen mansion stood near the Cumberland River. One afternoon in 1829 in the garden Mrs. Houston was told by a servant that a tall, strange man was in the reception hall and had asked to see her. As she entered the room she recognized Houston although he had disguised himself. He did not suspect that his secret had been learned and during their conversation spoke only of casual matters, but all the while he gazed at her steadily as if to stamp her face on his memory. He arose, made a deep bow, and left. Descending the bluff, he climbed into a canoe, and rowed away. Only an hour's ride distant was the Eagle Tavern, a famous stage hostelry a few miles southeast of The Hermitage. Other witnesses record that the night before Houston left for the West he stayed the night at the Eagle Tavern.

Davidson in the Thirties

The decade from 1830 to 1840 saw Tennessee and Tennesseans more prominent on the national scene than they had ever been. It was the Age of Jackson. Perhaps for this reason, there was less sensational action on the county stage. Events may be summed up in few words: the stars fell; the cholera scourged; financial panic frightened; Texas called; and the Whigs arose.

The population of Davidson County was 5566.

A Nashville merchant was governor when the decade began. Billy Carroll anticipated a later plank of the Whig platform: internal improvements. He proposed and the General Assembly passed in 1830 the Internal Improvements Act for development of roads and rivers. By the middle of the 1830s one result was the Hermitage Turnpike from Nashville east, replacing the old dirt road that had served since pioneer days with a macadamized highway. In 1831 a state prison was built in Nashville. On the Davidson County farms, wheat threshers were coming into use, reducing the amount of manual labor required and increasing yields tremendously, leading to the establishment of great flour mills. In 1834 a steam-powered rolling mill, with six boilers, opened near the upper ferry landing. In 1836 McEwen, Hayes & Hill began operating their new paper mill.

The corporate limits of Nashville had been extended in 1830, and a new post office became necessary in 1834. It was moved from the Public Square to the Colonnade Building on the corner of Cherry (Fourth) and Deaderick streets. During the 1830s and 1840s there were only two postmasters: Gen. Robert Armstrong (1829–1845) and Col. Leonard P. Cheatham (1845–1849). During this period also two noted lawyers flourished: Felix Grundy, who had been Chief Justice of Kentucky until removing to Nashville in 1807 and who was called "the ablest criminal lawyer in the Mississippi Valley" until his death in 1840, and Francis B. Fogg, one of the most admired public men of the decades before the Civil War. Davidson County was represented in the Constitutional Convention of 1834 by Fogg and Robert Weakley, a former U.S. Representative.

The prison was ready to receive guests on January 1, 1831. The first prisoner was from Madison County, a tailor sentenced to serve two years for assault with a knife. The prison was operated according to "the Auburn plan." Convicts occupied separate cells at night, but worked together in the day. There were a number of useful occupations offered: blacksmithing, picking wool, shoemaking, harness making. The intent was to teach the men a trade that they could use as law-abiding citizens. The public tended to be dubious. Nevertheless it was a progressive notion. Even more progressive was the decision to build a mental hospital near Nashville for the treatment of what the Act called "the most severe of earthly afflictions." This was in 1832 and $10,000 was appropriated; the building, designed by the architect Adolphus Heiman, was completed in 1840 after four times that amount had been spent. Strange to say there was much opposition to hospitalization of the mentally ill because of the cost to the taxpayer.

After the Medical Society of Tennesse had been established at a meeting of physicians in Nashville in 1830, a terrifying event focused public attention on health matters. Asiatic cholera swept over a filthy city. The city had incurred its very first public debt in 1830 when the corporation borrowed $50,000 to erect a waterworks. Physicians had been insisting that a contaminated water supply would encourage the spread of disease. But it was the disposal of waste that caused physicians to be even more apprehensive when Asiatic cholera came to seaboard cities in 1832. The disease appeared in Davidson County in December of that year, affecting the poorer, more congested sections first, the rural areas not at all. After 29 deaths the plague subsided, but from May 8, 1833, to June 17 it returned and raged without distinction of wealth or age. There were 83 deaths, including Josiah Nichol, president of the Branch Bank of the United States.

Jackson's reelection in 1832 continued the feeling at home that all was well, but there seemed to be a slowing down. Poeple did not really understand the banking crisis, but money did not seem to go as far.

Houston and Davy Crockett, San Jacinto and the Alamo had put Texas on everyone's lips but it was the financial crash of 1837 that sent many Davidson countians to Texas. On May 22, 1837, a meeting called because of increasing uneasiness over the trouble in the financial world of the Eastern states and chaired by Albert H. Wynne, discussed the probable suspension of specie payments by the banks. It was a complex situation aggravated by a worldwide credit crisis and the unfavorable balance of trade suffered by the United States. Banking crises tended to affect all parts of the commercial community and when crops in Davidson County (and Tennessee) failed in 1838 many farmers and small businessmen lost all they had. Their response was to seek better times in Texas, and in Arkansas and Louisiana. Others went West involuntarily.

The Cherokees who had resisted their tribal chiefs' decision to accept new land in the West were forcibly removed, under U.S. Army supervision. Their route, to become known as "The Trail Where They Wept" in Cherokee, or Trail of Tears, crossed Davidson County.

And in 1840, a presidential year, the rise of Whiggery in Tennessee was marked by the great Whig Convention, in the very front yard of Old Hickory. John Bell had been a leader in establishing the Whig party. He had been a member of the General Assembly in 1826 when he defeated the brilliant Felix Grundy in a race for the seat in the U.S. House of Representatives that later came to be called "the Hermitage seat." He eventually became speaker of the U.S. House, and split with Andrew Jackson mostly because of Van Buren's succession to the presidency. Beginning in 1834, Whiggery rose, its center in Middle Tennessee and in Knoxville, and in 1840 the party held its largest convention in Nashville. Electing William Henry Harrison that year and carrying Jackson's state overwhelmingly, the Whigs did not lose the state in a presidential contest until 1852. Davidson County was a stormy battleground each campaign, Democracy retaining a substantial body of support.

It was in 1833 that the natural phenomena known ever after as "the night the stars fell" occurred. Astronomers expect that from time to time the earth in its orbit will pass through great fields of meteors, pieces of rock or debris in space that when they strike the atmosphere will burn up because of friction. Not comets at all, the meteor showers will indeed appear from earth to be stars, rapidly moving out of their normal places in the heavens. There were so many to be seen on this night in 1833 that to the average watcher of the night sky it did appear that the heav-

The second Hermitage, built in 1819. (sketched reproduction of Charles Alexander Lesueur's 1831 sketch in the collection of the American Antiquarian Society)

ens were falling in a fiery shower upon the earth below and that the world was coming to an end.

Reflecting the great political excitement of the period was the rapid change in newspapers. The first daily newspaper in Davidson County was issued on November 23, 1831. It was the *National Banner and Nashville Advertiser,* and William G. Hunt was the editorial manager. On August 22, 1837, two newspapers, the *National Banner & Nashville Whig* and the *Nashville Republican & State Gazette,* were consolidated as the *Republican Banner,* a daily newspaper owned by Allen A. Hall and S. Nye, with C. C. Norvell as associate editor, handling the daily chores of news writing.

The most fashionable place of entertainment in the 1830s was Vauxhall Gardens, named for the similar resort in London. Located near Franklin Pike in the southern part of Nashville, it was owned by John Decker. There was a large and handsomely decorated assembly room, a promenade and walks, along which were set up booths for various amusements, and a circular railway, 262 yards in circumference, which was still remembered 60 years later. Cars ran on the rails propelled by the passengers who simply grasped a crank and turned it as rapidly as they wished to travel.

Mr. Zollicoffer's Town

Felix Kirk Zollicoffer was a resident of Davidson County for only a year more than half his life. During those 21 years, he stamped his name on the annals of county and town with such bold print that Nashville of the 1840s and 1850s was to bear the marks of his Whig philosophy as distinctly as it had borne the brand of Jacksonian Democracy for a generation.

A Greek Capitol

Tennessee had no designated permanent capital until 1843. The state constitution of 1796 designated Knoxville the capital city until 1802; after that date the legislature met in several places, including Nashville, but the new constitution of 1834 required designation of a permanent seat of government no later than the first week of the 1843 session of the General Assembly. The legislature that convened in October of 1843, after quite prolonged balloting, agreed on Nashville as the capital.

Once Nashville had been chosen as the permanent capital of Tennessee, the General Assembly authorized the erection of a suitably impressive capitol building. The sum of $10,000 was appropriated to begin construction. The elevation called Campbell's Hill was selected and acquired, the Corporation of Nashville purchasing the property for $30,000 and donating it to the state. Clearing of the land began on January 1, 1845, and the foundations were nearly finished by July. Edwin H. Ewing delivered the address at the laying of the cornerstone on July 4. The Nashville architect Adolphus Heiman had submitted a proposal for a Gothic Revival structure, but this had been rejected in favor of a Greek Revival building designed by the famous Philadelphia architect William Strickland.

Both Heiman and Strickland are responsible for some of Nashville's most distinguished buildings, the latter accepting a number of commissions while work on the capitol was in prog-

The state Capitol, William Strickland, architect, as shown on the Confederate States $20 bill.

ress. On April 7, 1854, Strickland died. His funeral services were held in the hall of the House of Representatives, which by that time had become a kind of town hall for the city's public occasions. His body was placed in a recess of the wall of the north portico. The last stone of the tower was laid on July 21, 1855; that of the lower terrace on March 19, 1859. The General Assembly had begun to meet in the building on October 3, 1853.

An Egyptian Church

One of Strickland's commissions was the third building of the First Presbyterian Church, on Church Street (since 1955 the Downtown Presbyterian Church). While the second building, erected in 1832 and destroyed by fire in 1848, had been in the classic Greek style, the Strickland design was Egyptian Revival. This had come into favor with architects, jewelers, and cabinetmakers after Napoleon's Egyptian campaign. The capitals of the

The Downtown Presbyterian Church, William Strickland, architect. Dedicated as the First Presbyterian Church on Easter Sunday, 1851. (sketch by unidentified artist on present church bulletin)

pillars on the front portico are lotus leaves; the winged sun of Heliopolis is repeated as a motif both in stone and in painted decorations. Brilliant interior colors heighten the geometric designs along the walls of the auditorium. It is altogether one of the most remarkable buildings in Tennessee, and is one of the few Egyptian Revival buildings still standing the United States. The cornerstone was laid on April 28, 1849.

The President Is Dead...

Andrew Jackson became dangerously ill in May of 1845, while Sam Houston was on a speaking tour delivering addresses on temperance and on the annexation of Texas, two major causes of the day. With his wife and son, young Sam, Houston wanted to reach Nashville before his beloved mentor died. Jackson had been ill for months, the ravages of tuberculosis finally overcoming the tough old man. He resolutely defied death long enough to write several letters, to Houston, to President Polk, to his old friend Francis P. Blair in Washington. He even sat for a portrait painter, George P. H. Healy. On May 29 the dying man received 30 visitors to his sickroom, taking each by the hand for farewell. The next day Healy showed the finished portrait to his approving model. To the last day Jackson maintained his alert interest in public affairs, in farm operations, in religion and the future life, and the welfare of The Hermitage people, white and black. The President died at 6 o'clock Sunday evening, June 8, 1845. Thirty minutes later the Houstons arrived. "My son," Sam Houston said, "try to remember that you have looked on the face of this great man."

The fifteen years after Nashville was selected permanent capital of the state were packed with events of note. There was the war with Mexico. And in 1847 the government powder magazine exploded; in 1849 there was a cholera epidemic which claimed as one victim former President Polk who died at Polk Place, his downtown mansion.

The national government produced its first postage stamps in 1847. Only seven local post offices in Tennessee were selected to issue the gummed stamps: these circled Nashville, perhaps as a compliment to President Polk. The next year Polk declined to ask reelection, and in the election of 1848, a military hero, General Zachary Taylor was nominated by the Whigs for the presidency. He won, and after his inauguration on March 5, 1849, Polk returned to Tennessee. He chose to take a roundabout way home, traveling by boat to Wilmington, Charleston, Savannah, and around into the Gulf and New Orleans, there taking a steamboat up the Mississippi River. During his stay in New Orleans he contracted cholera, which was again of epidemic proportions that year. Returning to Nashville and to his new home, the former residence of Felix Grundy on the corner of Union and Vine, he was given the best possible medical care, and, it is recorded, responded to treatment so that he had overcome the disease, but four days later, on June 15, 1849, he succumbed to weakness. Sarah Childress Polk continued to reside in the mansion until her death, one of the capital's most respected and influential citizens.

An American Bridge

In 1850 the first suspension bridge was built across the Cumberland River. The old covered bridge remained in place until the new one, 700 feet long, 110 feet above low water mark, was finished. The new bridge was planned by Adolphus Heiman, and the building contractor was Capt. M. D. Field, brother of the Cyrus Field who had superintended the laying of the first Atlantic cable. The first wire for the suspension bridge was stretched May 22, 1850; on June 28, the first horse and buggy crossesd over. At 6 P.M. on November 14, 1851, the old bridge fell, with a splintering crash, just after the laborers tearing it down had left work for the day!

An Italian Villa

But most representative of the prosperous decade were the fine homes that were built, of which the finest was Belmont. Isaac Franklin's death in 1846 left his young widow, Adelicia Hayes Franklin, the wealthiest woman in America. She was a descendant of the Bishops of Bath and Wells, and knew the courts of Europe. It is the influence of Le Petit Trianon that is felt most strongly at her new house. Furnishings of rosewood and mahogany, fine statuary of marble, a lavish formal garden in the manner of Tuscany, even a zoo and a deer park, embellished the villa. Windows, columns, decorative detail follow the pattern of the palace where Adelicia, now Mrs. Joseph A. S. Acklen, moved in the court of the Empress Eugenie. The main entrance, through which the students of Belmont College have been passing since 1951 and before them the young ladies of Ward-Belmont, consists of a recessed portico with two Corinthian columns forming three bays between the end projections that shape the recess. The columniation supports a cornice, above which is a parapet wall with statuary at the corners. On either side of the entrance are one-storey projecting porches. An octagonal observatory was placed atop the house. Belmont was completed in 1850.

Life and Death of a Public Man

Born in Maury County, killed in Kentucky, Felix Zollicoffer was brought back to the mourning city he called his own for burial with full military honors.

That the fiery editor's body was brought back to his town from the battlefield where he had lain dead, for a hero's funeral, in a Confederate general's uniform, and that the funeral was the last opportunity for the friends of the Confederacy to publicly display their loyalty to the cause before the fall of the city to Federal troops, simply secured his fame.

Of Swiss descent, Zollicoffer was born May 19, 1812, in Maury County, Tennessee. At 15 he became a printer's devil, apprenticed to his cousin, A. O. P. Nicholson, in his shop in Columbia. Two years later he was editor of a weekly newspaper at Paris, started with high hopes and slender resources by young Zollicoffer and two other teenagers. The enterprise failed, but Zollicoffer sold all he had including horse, saddle, and bridle, to pay its debts and become a journeyman printer. At 23 he finally became steadily employed with the *Knoxville Register* where he came under the influence of John Howard Payne (author of "Home, Sweet Home"). After marriage to Louisa Pocahontas Gordon in 1835 he settled down as an editor and publisher at Columbia, with time off in 1836 to fight in the Florida Seminole War. He also was appointed State Printer. A supporter of the Whig party, his opposition to Martin Van Buren was so effective that he became the leading Whig editor of the state. His support of James Chamberlain Jones for governor, putting him in opposition to Maury County's famous James Knox Polk, attracted such attention that he was called to Nashville in 1841 to take editorial charge of the Nashville *Republican Banner,* the state Whig organ.

The Whig campaign of 1844 sought to repeat the national triumph of 1840. Henry Clay was the standard bearer; the Democrats finally chose as a dark horse candidate James K. Polk. This made the Whig effort in Tennessee more important and more difficult. A large speaking ground was laid out near Nashville and on one August day a great parade was organized with hundreds of uniformed partisans from Davidson and other counties marching in companies to the speaking. Some were named "the Ashlanders," for Clay's mansion; others called themselves "Cedar Snags." One cavalry unit was named "the Horn Company" because every horseman carried a horn of tin, wood, or bone, which they blew lustily, as other paraders sang: "Come along, come along, Tennessee boys! Come along, come along, do! We'll open the way for Henry Clay, and Frelinghuysen too!" On a wagon pulled by six white horses was a loom, being operated by an expert woman weaver, indicated Clay's friendship for the working class. As the wagon moved along the line of march the woman wove cloth which Colonel Sam Morgan of Nashville tore off in strips and tossed to the onlookers. The largest delegation in the parade was awarded the prize of the day, a pink satin banner bearing a full-length portrait of Henry Clay.

Zollicoffer had become editor in 1842; he was appointed adjutant general of Tennessee by Governor Jones and then comptroller general. All Nashville came to know his ability and his personal magnetism. In August of 1849 he ran for the state Senate from Davidson County and was elected. In 1851, after a brief Democratic interlude under William Trousdale, Zollicoffer's powerful pen helped put William Bowen Campbell into the governor's chair and made the editor a national figure. He served as delegate to the Whig convention in Baltimore, at which Winfield Scott was nominated; Scott lost the election but carried Tennessee. During the heated campaign Zollicoffer was involved in an episode of violence that made him even more famous. It was the summer of 1852. The editor of his Democratic competitor was John Leake Marling. A new bridge was to be built across the Cumberland. There was controversy about the proper site. Marling favored the foot of Broadway, Zollicoffer and his newspaper favored a crossing from the corner of the Public Square. Marling suggested that the Public Square location offered opportunity for personal profit to the Whig editor and his friends. Several editorials were exchanged, tempers rose, and on the morning of August 20 Zollicoffer walked out of his Deaderick Street office to the corner opposite Marling's offices (in a building on the southwest corner of the present Fourth Avenue and Charlotte) and waited. Marling emerged, they stood on opposite sides of the street, and exchanged shots, both receiving wounds. (Both recovered and were reconciled.)

The next year Zollicoffer, nominated for the Congressional seat by the Whigs, was elected and served three terms. He supported the platform of the Southern Whigs and what came to be called the American Party: support of the Union, the Constitution, and enforcement of the laws, obvious code words for endorsement of the Dred Scott decision and the Fugitive Slave laws, the rock on which the late Daniel Webster's presidential aspirations had foundered. Such moderation was palatable to Davidson County voters; but their centrist position was increasingly untenable in a union moving toward disunion. In November of 1860, after the election of Lincoln, Zollicoffer wrote a friend that he opposed secession as a remedy; if the Southern states would meet in convention and formally request that the Federal government agree never to interfere with slavery as it existed in the several states, this would be a wiser and a better remedy. It was a singularly impractical and unrealistic notion. A more practical step, although the house of the Union was already afire, was the National Peace Conference which met in Washington on February 4, 1861, suggested by the legislature of Virginia. Zollicoffer and other moderates, including former President John Tyler, were delegates. Fort Sumter and the call to arms followed swiftly. Tennessee seceded in May; Zollicoffer was commissioned a brigadier in the Provisional Army of Tennessee, was assigned to the command of Camp Trousdale, and in July was sent to Knoxville as commander of Confederate forces in East Tennessee. In September his army advanced into Kentucky, fortifying Cumberland Gap, and on January 19, 1862, in the Battle of Mill Springs near Fishing Creek in Pulaski County, Kentucky, Zollicoffer was shot dead by Colonel S. S. Fry. Each officer, in the confusion of the battle, supposed the other to be of his own side and Fry was first to recognize the truth, firing his pistol at the Confederate general with mortal effect.

After the battle the general's body was removed to the Union camp. Dr. D. B. Cliffe of Franklin, Zollicoffer's brigade surgeon, was given permission to embalm it, and General George Thomas directed Surgeon Cliffe to transport the remains and those of Lieutenant Balie Peyton, Jr., to Nashville. On arrival, the general's body lay in state in the hall of the House of Representatives in the State Capitol, clad in dress uniform, his sword sheathed and lying upon the coffin, as hundreds of citizens and soldiers passed by. Bishop James Otey conducted Episcopal services and the funeral cortege wound down Capitol Hill and out to the City Cemetery where the body now lies. It was the last ceremonial act of Confederate Nashville and it closed an era in the story of Davidson County.

The Wool Champion of the World

Mark Robertson Cockrill (1788–1872) was another individual to stamp his achievements on this period of Davidson County life. In 1815, immediately after the Napoleonic Wars, it became possible to break the monopoly in breeding and raising Merino sheep thereto held by the Spanish monarchy. Mark Cockrill, born in a log cabin in Davidson County, was an enterprising young farmer tilling the acres conveyed to him by his father in 1811, when he sold the 210 acres that included some of the present Centennial Park and the rights to half the spring located just off the present West End Avenue, known as Cockrill's Spring, for money to buy thirteen head of Merino purebreds from a

flock near Washington, D.C. He drove them home himself, overland, and was in the wool business. Quality was Cockrill's goal:
"the first order of Broad Cloth wool." Wool and the hand loom
were the staples of Middle Tennessee agriculture. There was cotton, of course, but in the natural strife between cotton and wool
Davidson County was a sheep county. Cockrill's flocks numbered
in the thousands. Woolen broadcloth was the fabric of a gentleman's wardrobe and Cockrill's wool went into the very best
broadcloth. In 1835 he won a silver cup at the Kentucky State
Fair for "the best wooled sheep." (These were not Davidson
County born; all were natives of Cockrill's large estate near Can-
ton, Madison County, Mississippi. He sold it that very year for
$210,000 and came back home.) By 1848 he was urging hilly
Davidson and other Middle Tennessee counties as the ideal
ground for the Merino, which liked to ramble in places where
traditional row crop farming was difficult. He issued a head-on
challenge to German Silesia, which Europeans considered the
leading sheep and wool country. Competing at the Crystal Palace
Exposition in London in 1851 against wool from Silesia, Saxony,
Scotland, and all the other great wool-producing countries the
Davidson County product was pronounced the finest in the
world. "Nature gave me the advantage in climate," Cockrill said,
modestly.

The farm, called "Stock Place," in the decade before the war
offers a fair example of the significance of agriculture in the
economy of Davidson County in the nineteenth century. It consisted of 5000 acres about five miles west of Nashville on the
Charlotte Pike. The low ground was very productive; the up-
lands were rocky and less so. Where there was no rock the land
was fertile and was either tilled or sown in bluegrass. There were
3000 animals: 2300 head of sheep and the balance horses, mules,
and cattle. Most of the cattle were Durhams, but in 1856 Cockrill
had pioneered the raising of purebred Bates Shorthorns in Tennessee. To operate the farm he employed eight farmhands, six
men and two women. The wool clip of two years comprised
18,000 pounds of fine Saxony wool which was valued at 60 cents
a pound. He cultivated 120 acres of corn, 300 acres of oats, and

100 acres of wheat. The rest was in grass. The land was enclosed by a stone fence and the Cumberland River to the north. The farm supported a family of 40 persons; he later testified to Federal authorities that he had owned 98 slaves, presumably in addition to the farm hands and the "family," who were likely Cockrill's kin. This was not an uncommon extension in the Central South of that time, and later.

Golden Days

Many see the fifties as Davidson County's most glorious times. Certainly there were noteworthy events. In 1850 the Southern Convention met to discuss the slavery question and the national crisis, remaining in session 80 days. Jenny Lind appeared in concert under the management of P. T. Barnum. The first passenger train of the Nashville & Chattanooga railway in 1853 ran as far as Antioch. Ex-President Millard Fillmore visited in 1854, and the municipality of South Nashville was united with Nashville. But there were less desirable events too. During 1856–57 three great fires destroyed 22 buildings: March 16, 1856, 13 buildings on the Public Square; July 9, 8 more including the Masonic Hall; April 12, 1857, the courthouse and the historic old Nashville Inn. The Zollicoffer-Marling shooting affray of 1852 had not resulted in death to either, but in 1859 two other newspaper editors, Allen A. Hall and George Poindexter, shot it out on the street and Poindexter was killed.

On October 1, 1858, Randal William McGavock took the oath as mayor of Nashville. Thirty-four years earlier, another Randal McGavock, his uncle, had been mayor of a Nashville that contained 4500 persons—a large village or a small town—which no turnpike entered, still just a market town for the surrounding farms. Young McGavock presided over a city of 30,000, capital of a state with an imposing new capitol building, served by three railroads.

In 1858 Nashville was governed by a board of 8 aldermen and a council of 16. The mayor's duty was to send recommendations to the two bodies and preside over their joint meetings as the official head of the city, albeit a part-time functionary with little real power. (McGavock, as a matter of fact, practiced law throughout his term.) Nevertheless the mayor could exercise considerable influence and McGavock took pride in the street improvements, the building of Howard School, the meetings for railroad development, and above all in the new workhouse (in which religious services were held every Sunday afternoon). Before Nashville had any organized charity, he founded and was first president of the Robertson Association, a group of 20 who helped the poor and distressed during such emergencies as flood, drought, fire, and epidemic disease. Although McGavock declined to seek reelection in 1859 it was said of his administration years later that "there has never been one more anxious and thoughtful for the welfare and improvement of the city than Mr. McGavock."

Industrialization was fostered by the Whigs, wherever possible, but in some respects this kind of development was slow. Dr. John Shelby had opened a steam sawmill on the east bank of the Cumberland River in the early 1850s, and in 1864 Frank and Hugh McGavock were running another. A major engineering work of the period was the railroad bridge across the Cumberland, opened to traffic October 28, 1859. A drawbridge, it was built for the joint use of the Louisville & Nashville and the Edgefield & Kentucky railroads. The cost was $250,000, loaned the two companies by the State of Tennessee under the Whigs' general internal improvement laws. The bridge was 700 feet long, with two fixed spans and two draws. The engineer in charge could, it was claimed, turn the main draw into position in four and a half minutes.

And although the county seat was evolving into an industrial urban community, it was still the center of a rich agricultural region. True, the city covered six square miles and numbered 37,000 inhabitants (including suburban); true, the city was cosmopolitan with substantial German, Irish, Jewish, Greek, and Italian elements, besides those original Scotch-Irish, English, and French settlers' grandchildren, and the descendants of Africans; but there were still forests of hardwoods and cedars on the hillsides and in 1860 farmers of Davidson County raised

1,114,901 bushels of corn. The numbers of mules, horses, sheep, pigs, and cattle pastured on the lush grass presented a scene of agrarian contentment. This would end with the coming of war. And all the excitement of nationalistic patriotism, the bands, the flags, the high hopes would end with Zollicoffer's death. Buell's gunboats brought a new era.

Andrew Johnson's Town

In March of 1862 Andrew Johnson was made Military Governor of Tennessee. He took up his residence in Nashville. Ruling with an iron hand, imprisoning from time to time clergymen, physicians, elder statesmen, city officials, businessmen, and an occasional woman suspected of carrying contraband under her voluminous skirts (usually quinine or other medicines), Johnson was detested by all Davidson Countians who refused to take his prescribed loyalty oath. But after he became vice-president in January of 1865 and within six weeks president succeeding the assassinated Abraham Lincoln, his moderate plan for Reconstruction and his support of what came to be called in Tennessee the Conservative cause (backed by the popular former governor William Bowen Campbell) won the ex-Confederates over. For diametrically opposed reasons Nashville was from 1862 until 1873 Andy Johnson's Town.

Occupied City

Zollicoffer was killed at the lost battle of Mill Springs, Kentucky, on January 19, 1862. The Confederate right wing crumbled and was ordered back toward Nashville. On February 6 Fort Henry on the Tennessee River fell. The battle for Fort Donelson, its stronger mate on the Cumberland, began. On Sunday, February 16, Gen. George B. Crittenden's forces, retreating from Monticello, Kentucky, into Middle Tennessee by way of Livingston, crossed the Caney Fork at Trousdale's Ferry, 40 miles east of Nashville.

The panic which followed the realization that after Fort Donelson fell it would be only a matter of time before Federal troops would be marching into Nashville has never had a parallel.

The population knew that the battle at the fort on Sunday, February 16, would be decisive. Crowds gathered outside the *Union and American* office Saturday evening for bulletins. The next morning vague rumors began to spread, becoming more specific as they flew. Gen. Don Carlos Buell was at Springfield with 35,000 men. A flotilla of Federal gunboats was at Clarksville with orders to shell Nashville to destruction. Buell would be in Edgefield by sundown. And so it went—all false. But when John Miller McKee of the *Union and American* arrived at his office he found the city in a tumult. No calm voice could be heard. Inexplicably Confederate Governor Isham Harris, asked to issue a proclamation setting forth the true facts, declined to do so. Nothing was done to allay apprehension. It was as Rome must have been with the Goths at the gates. And it was such a beautiful, sunny day.

Services at the churches were either canceled or shortened and the pastors did not utter reassuring words: a hasty prayer and a quick exit was the rule. It was said that the governor had advised all women and children to leave the city by 3 A.M. Large numbers rushed toward the railroad stations, possessions under their arms or on their backs; they were mostly on foot for wagons or carts were not to be had. Earlier that day Gen. Albert Sidney Johnston had advised the governor to remove the state archives to a place of safety. The papers were packed and shipped to Memphis, probably on the same train that carried members of the General Assembly, which had gone through the formality of adjourning, to meet again in Memphis at the call of the governor. (The two houses had adopted a resolution authorizing this in a secret session held a few days previously.)

On Monday the Confederate headquarters realized that Nashville indeed could not be held. It must be surrendered. Crittenden's troops were ordered to change their line of march and head for Murfreesboro. The post office was closed (mail from the South was stopped at Murfreesboro, from Sunday). Two gunboats at the wharf were burned. (The pre-dawn blaze alarmed citizens who had heard the Texas Ranger troops swear they would burn Nashville to ashes rather than "turn it over to the Yankees.") On Tuesday, February 18, the Federal boats not having appeared, the distribution of Confederate government stores commenced, large amounts going to the citizens. Thousands of women, young and old, had been laboring for the government for several months without pay and they accepted payment of their due in this way, newspaperman McKee records. Despite protests from citizens who saw no reason for the act and much harm, the railroad bridge and the great suspension bridge that connected Nashville and Edgefield, allowing food supplies from the surrounding farms to come into the city, were destroyed by order of Gen. John B. Floyd, the former being burned and the cables of the suspension bridge being cut allowing it to collapse. Since the Federals were moving by water it was difficult to see the military necessity.

On Tuesday, February 25, the flotilla arrived. First to land were soldiers of the sixth Regiment of Ohio Volunteers, disembarking from the *Diana* preceded by their band playing "Hail, Columbia!" Their flag was hoisted above the state capitol, but soon another took its place. A native of Salem, Massachusetts, William Driver had lived in Nashville since 1837. He had gone to sea at the age of 14 and eventually became master of the *Charles Doggett*. During the voyage of this ship from Salem to New Zealand in 1831, Captain Driver began calling its starry flag "Old Glory." When he decided to retire from active sailing, he came to Nashville where his brothers Henry and Joseph had moved, bringing the ensign of the *Charles Doggett* with him, the original "Old Glory," and it was this large banner that he offered the Federal troops on the morning of February 27. They hoisted it to the top of the Capitol flagpole and it flew there all night, replacing the smaller regimental standard. Driver died in 1886 and was buried in the City Cemetery. By statute his grave is one place at which the flying of the national flag at night is authorized.

The Battles

A large part of the Union force in Nashville was withdrawn at the beginning of April of 1862. Actually the authority of the Military Governor encompassed little more than Davidson County. But on July 4 Johnson delivered one of the best speeches of his career. Speaking in Nashville to a crowd containing many who were for the Union but also were opposed to the abolition of slavery, he said: "I am for this government above all earthly possessions, and if it perish, I do not want to survive it. I am for it, thought slavery should be struck from existence and Africa swept from the balance of the world."

He thundered: "I believe, indeed, that the Union is the only protection of slavery—its sole guarantee; but if you persist in forcing this issue of slavery against the Government, I say in the face of Heaven, give me my Government, and let the Negro go!"

It was a cogent statement of the position Lincoln was to take consistently and which would form the foundation of the Lincoln-Johnson plan of Reconstruction. In all probability the speech made Johnson vice-president.

That spring Buell's troops had joined Grant at Pittsburg Landing and cavalry under Bedford Forrest and John Hunt Morgan was active everywhere; in May there had been a small battle with Morgan east of Nashville. On July 5 Confederate raiders surrounded the capital. In July Nashville was virtually cut off from communication with the North. General Braxton Bragg, planning to invade Kentucky, flanking the comparatively small force in the Nashville defenses, wanted to hamper the concentration of Buell's army. Forrest moved toward Nashville from Altamont, in the Sequatchie Valley. On July 13 he captured Murfreesboro; a garrison at Lebanon was hastily recalled to Nashville and the Federal commanders expected a full-fledged assault. Forrest had pulled back to McMinnville, then moved through Lebanon toward The Hermitage. Johnson impressed a thousand slaves from Davidson County farms to work on fortifications. Forrest observed the situation, decided not to press his luck.

Bragg's correspondence for the month of August in the *Of-ficial Records* plainly reveals that as late as August 11 his target was to be not Kentucky (where a battle was fought at Perryville in October) but Nashville. Bragg was then planning to proceed north from Sparta intending a frontal attack across Stone's River. But he changed his mind. On October 7, while Bragg's main force was in Kentucky, Confederate Generals S. R. Anderson and Bedford Forrest, with Governor Harris, who fancied himself a military leader, moved toward Nashville. The result was a battle at Lavergne, southeast of Smith Springs, a loss for the Confederates. On November 5 Forrest led a force of 8000 cavalry and infantry in an assault on the southen part of the city. This took place at 4 A.M. Two hours later, as it was becoming light, 1500 Confederate cavalry entered Edgefield, driving the Federal pickets before them. The railroad depot and machine shop and eight freight cars were destroyed. The railroad bridge, burned in the panic of February had been rebuilt and the attackers made an unsuccessful attempt to destroy it again before they withdrew. The fight lasted in all about ten hours. Confederate troops were moving south from the failed Kentucky campaign, toward Murfreesboro along the Cumberland and Stone's River turnpike. Union Gen. Thomas L. Crittenden's II Corps was moving south in parallel down the eastern edge of Davidson County and by the end of December Gen. William S. Rosecrans, who had replaced Buell at Johnson's insistence, was ready to act. Bragg had also convinced himself that Nashville was a soft apple ready to fall into his hands. The result was the Battle of Stone's River, a tactical draw but a strategic victory for the Union.

Not until October of 1863 would there be even a half-serious threat to the capital, although Confederate conscription was carried on right at Clover Bottom and around The Hermitage throughout the spring and summer. Letters stamped with Jeff Davis' picture were addressed to and delivered at Couchville, for example. In October Gen. Joseph Wheeler's cavalry conducted a large raid; in August of 1864 Wheeler again struck toward Nashville and on the night of August 29 cut Union communications within eight miles of headquarters. Urged to make an onslaught on the city Wheeler thought better of it and turned toward Alabama. In September Atlanta fell. Soon afterward Gen. John Bell Hood initiated his grand plan to strike a daring blow for victory.

There are those who insist that Gen. George Thomas won the Civil War on December 15–16, 1864. (An obscure officer named Gen. John F. Miller was in command of the post, but Thomas was field commander.) Hood marched north from Alabama, leaving Sherman to march to the sea; On November 30 a great battle was fought at Franklin. Hood's casualties in the frontal assault were enormous, not only in infantry but in the crucial area of field commanders. Federal troops retreated to the Nashville defenses. Thomas posted his army in a great crescent, its wings touching the Cumberland River at each end. On the afternoon of December 3 there was heavy skirmishing at the eastern side of the Federal line. The multitude on Capitol Hill, from which height the flashes of artillery fire beyond the Acklen residence (Belmont) could be plainly observed, stared fascinated. On the next day, Sunday, December 4, the Federal cavalry won a sharp fight on Hillsboro Pike. The two sides felt each other out for the next four days, but on Thursday night one of those snowstorms that so quickly come into Middle Tennessee blew in and snow fell furiously all day Friday. The next day, December 10, was characteristically sunny and crisp, and was used to prepare breastworks for the inevitable battle, but at dawn Tuesday the ground was covered with a thick shell of ice making it impossible to walk. A change in the wind to southerly warmed the earth and Thomas decided to attack on Thursday at 40 minutes after noon.

It was one of the major battles of the war. In spite of the disparity in numbers it was, like Waterloo, "a near thing." And in spite of the fierce charges and countercharges including the charge up Shy's Hill (between Hillsboro and Granny White Pikes), Hood lost not over 1500 in killed and wounded and Thomas not over 4000. The Union victory is reflected in the figure of 5000 Confederate soldiers taken prisoner. As the retreating army sang, it was all too true that "the gallant Hood of Texas

The Battle of Nashville monument stood on Franklin Road until damaged by a tornado in 1974. (sketch by Michael Birdwell from a photograph)

played hell in Tennessee." Large scale Confederate military resistance in the West ended with this defeat.

The city council, Union men all, appointed by Governor Johnson, passed a resolution thanking General Thomas for his able defense of the city and Brigadier General Donaldson, his aide, for the assistance he had rendered the corporation in obtaining provisions for the poor and in furnishing transportation.

As might have been expected in a wartime city filled with men far from home, prostitution was a major problem for both military and civil authorities. In the 1860 U.S. Census, 207 women gave their occupation as "prostitute." There may have been ten times that number during the Federal occupation. The soldiers frequented a section known as "Smokey Row." Thousands of soldiers were treated in Army hospitals for veneral disease. In early July 1863 a plan for deportation went into effect. The authorities rounded up 450 white women of the town, placed them on a steamboat and sent them elsewhere. The steamer went to Louisville. The authorities there forbade its landing. It proceeded to Cincinnati and met the same welcome. The Secretary of War ordered the boat back to Nashville and that ended the matter. The Provost Marshal pondered the problem and solved it, to his satisfaction at least. He instituted a plan for medical examination and licensing. The fees would support a hospital facility for rehabilitation. The plan succeeded.

A Lodging at the Union Hotel

In 1979 a number of miscellaneous old papers and books were being discarded at the Wilson County Courthouse in Lebanon. One of these books appeared to be a ledger, perhaps an exhibit in a forgotten civil lawsuit. Examination revealed it to be a hotel register, the register of the Union Hotel, E. W. Dandrige, proprietor, located on Market Street near the Nashville Public Square for the period of October 21, 1864, to July 7, 1865.

Most interesting are the pages covering the days of Hood's movement toward Nashville, November 30 to December 15. During this time there were guests from Cincinnati and Louisville, Chattanooga, Murfreesboro, Johnsonville, and Tullahoma.

Indiana, Michigan, Ohio, and Wisconsin are represented. A gentleman signed himself on December 11th as Jeff Davis of Richmond, Virginia, and he was accompanied by one John Barleycorn. Horace Greeley of New York purported to be a guest on December 29. On the day of the battle, December 15, however, there is a more puzzling registration: Lt. J. F. Watkins, 8th Tennessee cavalry, a regiment which was with Bedford Forrest at the time. In all, 308 guests registered between November 30 and December 15. There was no evidence of the panic that had gripped the city nearly three years before. An increasing number of known Middle Tennessee Confederates are listed on the register after January 1—one, J. H. Williams, who served with Wheeler's cavalry, inscribed a mocking verse poking sardonic fun at German soldiers in the Union Army. On April 20 an unknown hand wrote: "The Rebel Army is played out."

Reconstruction

For a time after peace was restored national troops remained in Nashville, the main encampment being marked by an enormous garrison flag. The appearance of the camp and the demeanor of the troops was not warlike. All were somehow relieved that it was over. Indeed, prosperity seemed to be the expected order. There was plenty of work for lawyers and doctors and teachers: deferred litigation filled the court dockets; new schools were being opened, in many cases with returning soldiers as teachers. Discharged men who had been preparing for a medical career came back to the University of Nashville and completed their studies. The Tennessee Conference of the Methodist Church met in October of 1865 and made pastoral appointments. One appointment was that of David Campbell Kelley, Bedford Forrests' second in command. Mrs. Robert Hatton, widow of a Confederate general, took her place in the Capitol: she was appointed state librarian. Davidson was an agricultural county—in the decade after 1860 the number of farmers increased by 40 percent while the average size of a farm decreased. Carpenters and bricklayers were in great demand. But Nashville had a new problem too.

The freedmen from farms in adjoining rural counties were moving to the city. For the first time Nashville began to have a residential section distinctly black in population, although there had been free blacks in the city before the war. There had been riots in Nashville in October of 1864 related to the coming national election, and as a result the McClellan slate of electors removed their names from the Davidson County ballot. During Reconstruction, the Ku Klux Klan, although active, was never the disturbing force that it was in the Deep South. It is said that the meeting that pulled together the scattered local bodies into the unified Southwide force was held at the Maxwell House. Davidson County Klansmen are reputed to have met in "konklave" in abandoned Fort Negley. One display of Klan force in Nashville occurred on March 5, 1868, when a mounted body hooded in Klan uniform rode along Church Street past the campus in an attempt to frighten the students of newly established Fisk University. In spite of this brief intimidation, the trustees kept the school open, the students stayed, and by the next year planning for a new campus began.

The Jubilee Singers

Thoughtful people, North and South, recognized the role that education would play in the lives of young black boys and girls. At Fisk in 1872 George White, who taught music, selected a dozen young people, gave them the name of Jubilee Singers, trained them in concert versions of the old slave songs (which he correctly perceived as songs of longing for freedom), and took them on a concert tour that began in humble village churches but ended eventually in the palaces of Europe.

Maggie Porter Cole, when she was an old woman in Detroit in 1935, recalled her childhood in the slave quarters of her Middle Tennessee farm home, how the workers coming home at dusk would raise their voices in the spirituals, how she was sent to the little school in Nashville, and how the Jubilee Singers took their melodies to the world. It is true that her voice was the greatest in that original group; that Mark Twain spent hours talking with her; that Madame Schumann-Heink, the celebrated German contralto, sat beside her in hotels in Paris and Berlin hearing her tell of the days "before the war;" that Gladstone wrote in her book that she "delighted his soul with music;" and that she sang before the Czarina of all the Russias while Grand Dukes applauded. But the most important thing the singers did was to put the value of black education before the general public. Members of that first tour were Minnie Tate, Green Evans, Isaac Dickerson, Jennie Jackson, Maggie Porter, Ella Sheppard, Thomas Rutling, Benjamin M. Holmes, and Eliza Walker. In a famous novel, *Chariot in the Sky*, Arna Bontemps, poet of the Harlem Renaissance and head librarian at Fisk for many years, has told their story.

Fisk University was founded in 1866 by representatives of the American Missionary Association and the Freedmen's Bureau. Its first classes were held in a former Union Army barracks and hospital on Church Street. In 1876 a new building in Gothic architecture was dedicated on a hill on Jefferson Street, to avoid the repeated floods that affected the original location. This building is called Jubilee Hall because the $150,000 needed to construct it was raised by the Jubilee Singers on their concert tours—the first college building in the United States to be paid for with money raised solely by student efforts. Jubilee Hall is now used as a residence hall and incidentally for teas, receptions, and weddings. The oldest building on the Fisk campus, however, is one of the Army barracks, which was moved there in 1873.

It had been on January 1, 1873, after the new campus of 25 acres was bought, that work on the foundations of the new building began—perhaps in commemoration of the effective date of President Lincoln's Emancipation Proclamation, ten years before to the day. And it was on the same day, exactly three years later, that the service of dedication was held, featuring an anthem, the music composed by James Merrylegs of Scotland with words from the Psalms. The architect of the building was Stephen D. Hatch of New York City.

It was not only the young black people of Davidson County who enrolled in that first class at Fisk: students came from all over the Central South, and many were older men and women (here again Fisk was a pioneer, for coeducation was uncommon) who saw the need and the advantage of becoming educated in a world of freedom.

Fisk was not the only institution for blacks opened in the postwar era. The Freedmen's Bureau also assisted in the establishment of Central Tennessee College in 1866, a joint effort with the Women's Missionary Society of the Methodist Episcopal Church. In 1874 funds to add a medical department to the college were provided by Hugh, Samuel, and Alexander Meharry. Central Tennessee College became Walden University in 1900. In 1916 the medical school received a separate charter as Meharry Medical College. In 1931 the medical school moved from its buildings on First Avenue South and Chestnut Street to the present campus near Fisk. A third black institution, Roger Williams University, was established in 1874 by Baptists on 21st Avenue South, a site acquired in 1910 for George Peabody College for Teachers.

Bankruptcy

Reconstruction was a time of recovery, but it was also a time for opportunism. Government with its easy access to the public purse offered a tempting field for looters. The appointment of Augustus E. Alden, a northern newcomer, as mayor of Nashville in 1867 aroused the barely concealed wrath of traditional community leaders. Old party names had lost their meaning: not all who had supported the Union cause in Davidson County supported the Republican cause—the Radicals, as they called themselves. Nor had all who now opposed the Republicans been Democrats, many had been Whigs; therefore the Radical opposition called themselves Conservatives. And, finally, only a minority of Radicals could properly be called "Carpetbaggers"— transplanted northerners. There were native Tennesseans, like Gov. William G. Brownlow and Gen. William B. Stokes, who gloried in the name of Radical. Alden, however, was from the North, a Republican Radical, and hated. He was also progressive, in the best sense: free public education for black and white, municipal welfare programs, and necessary public works construction projects were undertaken by the Alden administration. Economy, however, was not a high priority. Expenditures were twice receipts. The wealthier property owners became disturbed. A Tax-Payers Association was formed at the suggestion of Dr. J. Berrien Lindsley, with a Union man, H. G. Scovel, as president. In the spring of 1869 Col. A. S. Colyar, Judge Joseph Conn Guild, and former Gov. Neill S. Brown were appointed a committee to apply to the chancery court for a decree placing the city government in the hands of a receiver and an injunction forbidding the city officials from exercising any further authority or making any further expenditures. It was an unprecedented step. Chancellor Charles G. Smith granted the decree and appointed John M. Bass receiver. His required bond was $500,000. The largest property owners in Nashville, including six black men, signed the bond. By October the restrictions on suffrage had been removed and, with men enfranchised who had not been able to take the required oath that they "had not served the Confederacy nor sympathized with it"during the war, K. J. Morris was elected mayor with a satisfactory board of aldermen. One of three commissioners elected in 1870 was a black man, Randall Brown, the first to hold elective office in Davidson County.

"Entrenched in the Hearts of the People"

In 1872 Andrew Johnson came to Nashville again. There was a Democratic Party state convention to nominate a candidate for Congressman-at-Large. A political friend met with the ex-president in his room at the Maxwell House. Johnson explained to him that there was considerable pressure on him to become a candidate but he was reluctant because he was making careful plans to run for the Senate seat three years later. "If my name is put in nomination, promptly withdraw it on my authority," he instructed. This happened, and Gen. B. F. Cheatham was nominated the Democratic candidate; Horace Maynard was the Republican nominee. But under continued pressure from friends, Johnson the next day stood in the Public Square in Nashville and announced that he would be an independent candidate. The

Resembling the striped brickwork of Keble College, Oxford, is the Petway Reavis Building on Church Street, its distinctive face unnoticed by passersby who do not look up.

canvass that followed was remarkable for its eloquence and lack of malice. Maynard won, but Johnson did what he had planned: secured the election of a General Assembly favorable to his Senate hopes and his vindication of the congressional impeachment charges. Said the *New York Times:* "He is more firmly entrenched in the hearts of the people . . . than at any time since 1860." The hatred with which Occupied Nashville had regarded Andy Johnson when he was total military dictator of city and county had turned to admiration and love.

In the early winter of 1875 the General Assembly was to elect a United States Senator. Johnson realized his ambition. After a fiery canvass of the state and backed by 35 solid votes that would not be swayed, Andrew Johnson was returned to the Senate. He defeated three former Confederate generals and a respected former Whig candidate for governor, Gustavus A. Henry. At the Capitol the crowd that had packed the legislative chambers when the last of 55 ballots was taken rushed into the downtown streets cheering, marching to the Maxwell House. He spoke to a crowd of ten thousand on the Public Square in the evening, as the champion of mercy and justice for the South. A Johnson biographer, Lloyd Paul Stryker, asserts: "No oration in his whole career was comparable with this and at no time did he seem greater."

Cholera!

Although Davidson County was described in a brochure for a college in the 1840s as "healthful" this was not quite true. There were serious health problems, often reaching epidemic proportions: not the mosquito of the Mississippi valley, but the poor sanitation of a community living on a shelf of limestone. Cholera had been the most lethal scourge. This violent intestinal infection first entered the United States from the Orient in 1832. A year later it swept into Middle Tennessee, reaching its deadly peak in June; again in 1834 it came, and in the early summer of 1835. Previous plague years were surpassed in 1849 when 311 died including the recent president of the United States, James Knox Polk. Cholera came back to Nashville in 1854 as recorded in a letter a Texan received from his father in Tennessee: "It has been one of the sickliest springs and summers I have ever witnessed since the cold plague in 1816, and a great many deaths of cholera, typhoid, measles, the flux, and other diseases."

Remarkably the county was not visited by cholera in epidemic form during the war years. But in 1866 recovery was impeded by a cholera epidemic of great severity. The dreadful climax came in 1873. Business was beginning to flourish. The county's population was increasing. But in May of what was a hot, early summer, the first case of cholera was diagnosed in Nashville. On June 8 the disease was epidemic in proportion. The exodus to the hills began. Dr. William K. Bowling noted a strange fact: "Cholera shuns the country where malaria abounds. Columbia, 40 miles south of us, with its annual chills and fever, was never visited by cholera, while Lebanon, amid her majestic cedars and innocent of chills, is terribly scourged by it." June 20 came to be known as "Black Friday." Coaches traveling to the Cumberland mountains, where health prevailed, had been crammed full of frightened families for days. Hundreds perished before the epidemic abated. Dr. Bowling forbade his patients to eat fresh fruits and vegetables. He began to suspect the truth: cholera was conveyed in water, raw milk, raw vegetables and fruit, most frequently when contaminated by the common housefly.

This then was a watershed. Although it would be years before the events of the great war and occupation, first by an army, then by spoilsmen, would be forgotten, and although the transition to a financial and transportation center was so slow that those living then hardly noticed, after 1873 Nashville was no longer the occupied city, ruled by Andrew Johnson. On July 31, 1875, its military governor from 1862 to 1864, but its choice for United States Senator in 1874, died at his home at Greeneville. Perhaps no other man in Tennessee history had so reversed his public image.

A Southern Courthouse Town

This is the period from 1873 to 1908, the time of dreams of the "New South," of a town left in the backwaters when the floodwaters of occupying armies, carpetbaggers, and wartime profiteers and speculators had receded. It was an era of railroads and red brick warehouses and factories, of trade and transport, of bonds and stocks, of telegraph and electric light bulb, the new telephone, halftone engravings in the *Nashville Banner,* leisurely summer afternoons, and misty autumn evenings. Through it all Nashville remained a southern courthouse town.

Civic Leaders

Samuel Dold Morgan is entombed in the State Capitol, in an alcove in the southeastern corner of the building. He had been chairman of the committee that designed and erected it. To his committee he announced at once: "Some of you want to build only a large brick barn. I will not have it."

Born in 1798 in Staunton, Virginia, he came with his family to Blount County as an infant, and then to Huntsville, Alabama. After attending the University of Nashville, he became a resident of the city in 1833. He entered the wholesale dry goods business and actively participated in the erection of textile mills. He may be called Nashville's first industrialist. He was an ardent Whig from the beginning, participated in the great Whig parade in Nashville in 1844, and remained loyal to the Union. After Fort Sumter, however, he strongly supported the Southern cause, establishing a factory in Nashville to manufacture percussion caps used by the Confederate Army in the victory of First Manassas. When Nashville was occupied he moved his factory farther south and continued to supply caps throughout the war. After his death on June 10, 1880, the shops and factories of the city were closed at noon on the day of the funeral.

It is surprising that the name of Thomas A. Kercheval (1837–1915) is almost forgotten. Mayor of Nashville from 1872 to 1887, with the exception of two brief interruptions when Democrats were elected, the "Red Fox," as Kercheval was known, retained power against both the old Confederates and the New South business progressives. He apparently used an alliance of white labor, blacks, Irish immigrants, and white Republicans to fashion a ward-based political organization like those running northern cities. Born at Fayetteville, he came to Nashville during the Federal occupation and became a clerk in the Provost Marshal's headquarters. He read law and was admitted to practice, taking leadership of the Republican party as a Radical during Reconstruction. In 1867 he was elected to the state Senate, was reelected, became a member of the city council, and in 1872 won his first term as mayor. In 1874, a Democrat, Morton B. Howell, unseated him, but he came back in 1875 and remained mayor until 1883. A reform movement carried the election that year, which also marked the beginning of two-year terms for the mayor. The business candidate, C. Hooper Phillips, served from

Built in 1886 and demolished in the 1960s, Tarbox School was a red brick structure on Broad Street near Division. There were eight grades with promotions twice a year. Many successful men and women of Davidson County still remember their years at Tarbox with affection. (sketch by Michael Birdwell from a 1960 photograph)

1883 to 1885, when Kercheval returned. He finally yielded the office in 1887, when he became a member of the Board of Public Works.

The best that can be said of Kercheval's administration is that he maintained a status quo, neither going hopelessly into debt nor reducing city services. He was an unashamed partisan of the Republican administrations from Ulysses Grant to Benjamin Harrison at a time when the spoils system flourished. And he was a friend of laborers as well as the saloonkeeper, of the black and the poor white as well as the ward heeler. The business class, the former Whigs, and the old aristocracy were Democrats in Bourbon Davidson County—and they disdained the Red Fox and his followers.

But former Confederate officers also held positions of leadership during this period, of whom Benjamin Franklin Cheatham may have been the most famous. Cheatham was born in Nashville in 1820 and served in the Mexican War as, successively, a captain, a colonel, and, as the war ended, a general of Tennessee Volunteers. When gold was discovered in California in 1849, he went West, but soon returned to Nashville.

At the outbreak of the Civil War, Cheatham offered his services to the state and was appointed a brigadier general, ending the war as major general. He had been a personal friend of General Grant during the Mexican War and they resumed their friendship after 1865. During Reconstruction he was a strong voice for stable government and restoration of suffrage to the Confederate soldier. When the Democrats regained power under John C. Brown and James D. Porter, Frank Cheatham was named Superintendent of State Prisons in 1875. After Grover Cleveland became president he was named postmaster of Nashville in 1885; he died in September of 1888.

Samuel Watkins was a man whose services after his death have been greater than those during his lifetime, because of the bequest that established the Watkins Institute. He was born in or about 1794 in Virginia. He was a foster grandchild of James Robertson. He served in the Creek War and at New Orleans, then learned the brickmaking trade, and from 1827 to 1861 was a prominent builder. He acquired a large farm near the city on the Hillsboro Pike. Although he was not in favor of the war he lost greatly by its destructive events; part of the Battle of Nashville took place on his land. Because he was not for secession he was made superintendent of the gas company in 1862 and he rose to be president of the Nashville Gas-Light Company. After his death in 1880 a bequest of $100,000 and a lot at High (now Sixth Avenue North) and Church streets provided for the establishment of a free school, at first for the poor, but soon for the general adult public, called Watkins Institute. This unique institution plays a key role in adult education in modern Davidson County.

The first woman physician of Davidson County was Dr. Clara

Union Station from a post card of 1922.

C. Plimpton, a graduate of the New York Homeopathic College. She located in Nashville in 1878 and was successful in her practice and as attending physician at the Woman's Hospital.

Railroads

One of the most prominent names in the development of the railroads that were to be the main dynamic force behind Davidson County's growth during the 35 years following 1873 was Edmund W. Cole. He arrived in the city in 1845, 18 years old, a Giles County farm boy, and without a cent. Employed as a clerk in various kinds of stores for three or four years, he finally was accepted as a bookkeeper for the post office. This experience after several years got him the same job with the Nashville & Chattanooga Railroad, founded in 1848 by Vernon K. Stevenson. Cole became superintendent of the line in 1857; president in 1868, after the company had endured stirring times during the Civil War. During the next four years he acquired four small lines. In 1873 he renamed the line the Nashville, Chattanooga, & St. Louis Railroad, known to all Davidson County as the "N.C. and Saint L" or just the "ennancee."

The Louisville & Nashville Railroad, much larger and a part

of the August Belmont empire, bought Stevenson's controlling interest in 1880. Cole resigned and entered the banking business. His sudden death on May 25, 1899, at the Fifth Avenue Hotel shocked the city.

Athens of the South

In the fall of 1871, in Lebanon, at the meeting of the Tennessee Annual Conference of the Methodist Episcopal Church, South, Dr. David Campbell Kelley handed a resolution to the secretary. It was a declaration that a committee should be named and directed to visit at least seven other Conferences with the stated purpose of looking to the creation of a university of high grade and large endowment within the boundaries of the Conference. The resolution being adopted the committee named included Dr. Kelley, Dr. R. A. Young, and Dr. A. L. P. Green. The result of their efforts was a decision to locate The Central University of the Methodist Episcopal Church, South, in Nashville. Through the efforts of Bishop Holland McTyeire Commodore Cornelius Vanderbilt gave $500,000 for this purpose. Soon after he gave a second equal sum, and his son, William H. Vanderbilt, added another half million. The university was then named Vanderbilt University. It opened for classes in 1873. Dr. Young was elected secretary of the Board of Trust for seven years. The first four years of his term were devoted to buying and improving the campus at the end of Broadway, south of West End Avenue, and putting up numerous buildings.

In 1875 another newly formed school came into the estate and buildings of the University of Nashville. The story is quite complicated.

During the administration of Dr. Philip Lindsley from 1825 to 1850 the University of Nashville (whose name had been changed in the former year from Cumberland College) was respected intellectually but starved financially.

Philip Lindsley's son, John Berrien Lindsley, succeeded him. A medical department was opened and within a decade was the third or fourth largest in the country. In 1854 the Western Military Institute became the military department. It prospered.

Old Central, on the Vanderbilt University campus, was a fine city residence before there was a university. It eventually became home of the Department of English.

The literary department, reopened in 1855, struggled until the Civil War. The school was then closed but in 1870 it was organized as a military college by Gen. E. Kirby Smith.

When the George Peabody Fund became involved in the affairs of the University of Nashville in 1875 at the invitation of the state, a new organization became imperative. Eben S. Stearns was elected president.

The literary department of the University of Nashville was, in effect, converted into what was first called the State Normal College. The preparatory department, created by a bequest in the will of Montgomery Bell and called Montgomery Bell Academy, became virtually a separate operation. The academy had opened in the former literary department buildings in 1867.

What was officially called the State Normal College of the University of Nashville was established by the General Assembly of the state in 1875 and on December 1 of that year this institution was inaugurated. The enabling act amended the charter of the University of Nashville and, by implication, directed the trustees to discontinue the College of Arts, and to make an arrangement with the trustees of the Peabody Fund to establish a normal school for the professional training of teachers.

Dr. Stearns served as president until his death in 1887, when he was succeeded by Dr. William H. Payne. By 1880 the school had become the State Normal College, and then in 1889 the Peabody Normal College. On November 21 of that year the Peabody trustees, including former President Rutherford B. Hayes, came to Nashville, meeting on the campus for the first time.

Under Dr. Payne the school grew vigorously until 1901. Paul K. Conkin, in his 1985 history of Vanderbilt, details concisely the moves of Chancellor James H. Kirkland to arrange an "affiliation" between Peabody and Vanderbilt by which the teachers' college would be a part of yet separate from Vanderbilt. This was an ingenious idea which was quietly broached during a period of transition for the normal college. The timing may not have been a coincidence.

However other forces were moving and the devious scheme of Kirkland did not mature. James D. Porter, chairman of the board of trustees of the University of Nashville, was chosen as the new president of Peabody Normal College. He was 72. He was opposed to moving the school from its South Nashville campus to one close to Vanderbilt, a site on 21st Avenue South made available by the trustees of Roger Williams University, which had ceased operation. Once the move was approved, he resigned, in 1909.

The status of the school at this time is difficult to explain because the legal entities overlapped somewhat. In 1903 the University of Nashville consisted legally of these components: the Peabody College including the Winthrop Model School; the Medical College; the Conservatory of Music; the Montgomery Bell Academy.

The medical department of the University of Nashville had been organized in 1850. It was reconstituted in 1867. In 1874 it became known officially as "The Medical Department of the University of Nashville and of Vanderbilt University." The faculty and classrooms were the same. Degrees were confirmed in the name of each institution. This arrangement was terminated in 1895. Vanderbilt erected its own building; most of the faculty stayed in what then was called The Medical School of the University of Nashville. In 1909 this combined with the University of Tennessee medical school.

So in 1909 George Peabody College for Teachers was chartered; in 1911 Bruce Ryburn Payne accepted the presidency. Instruction ceased on the old campus, and in 1914 it was resumed in three new buildings on the new. (There is no adequate history of the University of Nashville; therefore, this account is offered in detail in an attempt to partially fill the gap.)

One premier institution was lost in 1877, when the Nashville Female Academy closed. Founded in 1816, Dr. Daniel Barry was its first principal, succeeded by Dr. R. A. Lapsley, Dr. W. A. Scott, and Dr. C. D. Elliott, who served from 1840 until 1877. In 1860 this was the largest women's college in the United States with 513 students and 38 teachers. The building, on Church Street, was badly damaged during the Federal occupation, but the school did reopen, although on a much smaller scale. The depression of 1873 affected its prospects severely. Litigation having its origin in personal animosities and possibly covetousness was fatal.

Centennials

There were two great celebrations during this period. The first was the celebration of the one hundredth anniversary of the founding of Nashville. On May 20, 1880, the equestrian statue of General Andrew Jackson by Clark Mills, the famous sculptor, was unveiled as the chief event of Nashville's Centennial. During the 1870s a large terrace had been laid out east of the Capitol. The Jackson statue was the centerpiece of this terrace. In 1879 the Tennessee Historical Society had learned that the work by Mills was for sale. There were three: one now stands in Jackson

Square in New Orleans, and the second in Lafayette Square, across from the White House, in Washington. Mills told the crowd it was "the first equestrian statue ever poised on hind feet in the world and the first ever modeled and cast in the United States." He said that he considered the Nashville statue the most perfect of the three. The Capitol was decorated with streamers and garlands and a temporary triumphal arch was erected over the main gate (then located at the southeast corner of the grounds). The crowds packed every part of the terrace, thronged to the porticoes, and hundreds sat precariously on the roof. Two young ladies were seen to climb out of a window of the second floor and perch confidently on the narrow ledge outside from which they could obtain a better view. In 1884 a marble base replaced the temporary wooden pedestal of the statue, appropriately, as the city's first charter was granted in 1784.

Tennessee had been admitted to the Union in 1796. Therefore there was much interest in a centennial exposition to be held in Nashville, modeled on the great Chicago World's Fair of 1892, but on a smaller scale. In 1894 an association was formed to prepare an exhibition of the arts, sciences, inventions, resources, and products of the state. Industrial recruitment and development was the goal to be kept foremost in mind; Tennessee would put its best foot forward. Difficulties arose and the opening was postponed from 1896 but on May 1, 1897, the Exposition formally opened, with cannon firing, flags waving, fireworks, speeches by Gov. Robert L. Taylor and others, and electrical generators turned on by the pressure of a button in the White House by President William McKinley. (Later the President, his wife, and a large delegation came to Nashville on Ohio Day.) The official attendance on opening day was recorded as 20,175. The grounds gleamed. There were 34 white buildings in a setting of green grass, small lakes, flower beds, walks winding through the trees; altogether, the newspapers said, "an enchanted city." Calling it "Centennial City," E. C. Lewis, the director general, presented a key to Major John W. Thomas, president of the Centennial Company.

The Parthenon represents Nashville as "The Athens of the South." The original replica of a Greek temple was the central building of the Tennessee Centennial Exposition of 1897. In 1931 it was rebuilt in permanent form, under the supervision of Wilbur F. Creighton.

The Carmack Tragedy

Edward Ward Carmack was born near Castalian Springs in 1858, but came to reside at Columbia in Maury County. He was a lawyer but was drawn, as many lawyers are, toward journalism and politics; indeed, the three professions are symbiotic. In 1886 Col. Duncan Cooper, publisher of the Nashville *American*, needed an editor for his newspaper and, impressed by young Carmack's record in the legislature, asked him to take the job. Later Carmack founded the Nashville *Democrat*, and when it was merged with the *American* he became editor-in-chief of the combined papers. In 1892 he was hired as editor of the Memphis *Commercial* and plunged into city politics there. In Nashville, he had been a spokesman for the Regular Democrats and Senator Isham G. Harris, a Memphian. He also became interested in the cause of temperance and reform. After the congressional election of 1894 had proven disastrous for the Democrats, Carmack wrote: "Unquestionably, the Democratic Party has failed to meet the wishes of the people." His recommendation was that the Democrats embrace the cause of free silver and economic reform. Memphian Josiah Patterson, the incumbent congressman, was a "gold bug." It was inevitable that the fiery, ambitious Carmack would challenge him, and in 1896 he defeated Patterson and went to Congress. He served there until 1901 when he was chosen to succeed Harris in the Senate. Malcolm "Ham" Patterson, son of Josiah Patterson, succeeded Carmack as congressman from the tenth district.

Defeated for reelection to the Senate by Robert L. Taylor, Carmack then looked toward the governorship. Ham Patterson and Ned Carmack were natural rivals. Carmack had become an ardent supporter of the prohibition of the sale of intoxicating liquors. In speeches and editorials he advocated the enactment of a statewide prohibition law (a "four-mile" law provided de facto local option). Patterson was backed by some of the party establishment and the powerful liquor interests—distillers, brewers, wholesalers, saloonkeepers—in the 1908 Democratic primary. He won the nomination in a bitter contest.

Carmack then became editor of *The Nashville Tennessean* (formed by the merger of the *Democrat* and the *American*) and continued the battle. With a vigorous editorial pen, he exposed a number of dubious transactions involving friends of the administration. One of his targets was Col. Duncan Cooper of Nashville. On Sunday, November 8, 1908, an editorial appeared in the *Tennessean* entitled "Across the Muddy Chasm," a personal attack on Cooper, who then remonstrated and thought he had received an assurance that his name would not appear again. On Monday another editorial, "The Diplomat of the Zweibund," mentioning Colonel Cooper, was published. That evening, as Carmack walked along Seventh Avenue North between Union and Church streets, he encountered Colonel Cooper and his son Robin. Shots were fired and Carmack was left for dead on the sidewalk. Duncan Cooper was tried and convicted. The case

Gables, turrets, and late Victorian stained glass mark the Romanesque Revival building of the Lindsley Avenue Church of Christ, built in 1894 as Grace Presbyterian Church.

against his son was not pressed. After the Tennessee Supreme Court confirmed the sentence, Colonel Cooper was greeted by the warden at the gates of the state penitentiary with a pardon signed by Governor Patterson. The public outrage was so great that in January 1909 a statewide prohibition law passed over the governor's veto. The Democratic party was split, and Patterson's political career never recovered.

Vanderbilt Football—Glory Days

Between 1902 and 1913 the Vanderbilt football team was beaten by only four teams: Cumberland University, the University of the South (Sewannee), Michigan, and Ohio State. During these twelve years games against all other schools ended in victory for the Commodores. And one of those defeats led directly to the employment of the man whom many remember, over fifty years later, and regard as a genius of the game—Dan McGugin. It was the 6–0 loss to Cumberland in 1903 that smarted. The

"Big Four" in Southern football were Vanderbilt, Sewanee, Clemson, and Cumberland. After the defeat, in Nashville, John Edgerton, Vanderbilt captain, who was from Lebanon, lay on the ground and wept. "I can't go home now!" he muttered. Beating Sewanee later was no compensation: Clemson and Cumberland played in Montgomery, Alabama for the Southern championship that Thanksgiving, the first postseason game played in the South.

On February 15, 1904, McGugin was hired, and the glory days began, never to be forgotten.

A Time For Reform

The period from 1909 to 1925 was dominated in Davidson County by two influences: reform and war. The First World War shook the county in every way, economic, cultural, social, and political, although the political effects were not so much a product of the war crisis as of a realization that Nashville was losing ground to its more aggressive rivals, Memphis, Birmingham, and Chattanooga. The structure of government needed change. It was Hilary Howse, elected by the Democratic Regulars in a struggle with the reform faction, whose personality dominated the era.

Before Hilary Howse was elected mayor in 1909, the city of Nashville had been embroiled in political turmoil, the product of strife between the new commercial and financial class and those who preferred a status quo dominated by ward politics. This was a complex controversy. It involved the strong tide of civil and moral reform that had been rising nationally since the scandals of the Grant presidency. Locally it was sometimes called the "Good Government" movement, or "Goo-Goos," as its foes sneered.

But Who Shall Be Our Leader?

Hilary Howse was born in 1866 in Rutherford County and stayed on the farm until he was 18. He said he came to town with thirty cents in his pocket (actually, "three borrowed dimes").

Thoroughly Italian in appearance with its red tile roof, yellow brick, and campanile, the Cathedral of the Incarnation has a beamed ceiling decorated in gold leaf, the first of its kind in the United States. The building was dedicated in 1914.

After working as a clerk in a furniture store, he and his brother Kai Howse in 1900 opened their own store. His rise in politics began with a seat on the county Democratic executive committee. He won a seat on the county quarterly court in 1900, won a seat in the state Senate in 1905, and again in 1907. He supported legal betting on horse races (Cumberland Park was a flourishing racing establishment), and Malcolm Patterson's run for governor, always opposing prohibition.

Between 1887, when Republican rule ended with the resignation of Thomas A. Kercheval, and 1909, Nashville had nine different mayors. Charles P. McCarver had resigned in 1890, and was succeeded by William Litterer, who served until George Guild was elected in the fall of 1891. Guild was reelected in 1893 but William M. McCarthy, a Good Government candidate (supported by the anti-immigrant, anti-Catholic American Protective Association) won in 1895. The Democratic "Regulars" and the Nashville Irish joined forces in 1897 to elect Richard Houston Dudley. James M. Head, a lawyer, former owner of the Nashville *American*, a progressive but not a reformer, succeeded Dudley in 1899. He served two terms and was succeeded by Albert S. Williams in 1903, who was succeeded by Thomas O. Morris in 1905 and James S. Brown in 1907. The Committee of One Hundred, which wanted reform in government but wanted social reforms even more, played a major role in these shifts. Regrettable to say, money from saloonkeepers and gamblers also played a role, and the price for their support was a wide-open town. The political panic that followed the death of Carmack led to statewide prohibition. To counter this fearsome threat, Hilary Howse, running for mayor in 1909, exploited the natural resentment of the citizenry against compulsion and the resentment of liquor dealers at loss of profits. In an often-quoted statement he said: "As long as I stay in a free country I will eat and drink as I please." Howse carried every ward in the primary. In the general election on October 14, 1909, he defeated Charles D. Johns, a former sheriff running on a strict enforcement platform, two to one. For the next fifteen years the person of Hilary Howse was to be the principal issue in local public affairs.

The ouster of Howse in 1915, under new state legislation, was caused by deficits and other budget problems which raised the ire of the civic reform faction whose chief deity was fiscal responsibility. A new city charter installing a commission plan of municipal government had been adopted in 1913: popular at the time, it soon proved to be the most chaotic and unworkable method of government possible. Howse regained the mayor's chair in 1925 and served until his death in 1938.

1918: Year of Trouble, Year of Triumph

There had been two catastrophes during the decade: soon after midnight on November 5, 1912, a corner of the city reservoir on Kirkpatrick Hill cracked, spilling more than 25 million gallons of water. No lives were lost, but there was much property damage to homes and buildings; the aftermath shook the foundations of municipal government as well. On March 22, 1916, a fire destroyed more than 900 buildings in East Nashville. There was one death, 3000 persons were without shelter, and an area from First to Tenth streets was left scorched.

Then the morning of July 9, 1918, a trainload of workers at the powder plant at Old Hickory was inbound. Proceeding at speed, it collided head-on with another N.C. & St. L. train, westbound on the same track at a curve near White Bridge Road: 101 died. The wreck at Dutchman's Curve is still the worst in the loss of life in American railroad history.

The powder plant was the major war industry in the county. In 1917 the DuPont Corporation of Wilmington, Delaware, obtained a government contract to manufacture smokeless powder. The plant built at Old Hickory had a capacity of 700,000 pounds per day. A company town (Dupontonia) was built: over 10,000 construction workers of the Mason-Hangar Company worked on the project. The plant was in production only eight months before the war ended; afterward DuPont established a plant to manufacture cellophane and rayon, an early venture into synthetics, that maintained Old Hickory as a major industrial complex for another half century, one of the six largest payrolls in the county.

Stanley Horn, a Nashville businessman (also noted historian and writer) recalled: "They had 56,000 men (and women) on the payroll and they were recruited from everywhere. The plant was so big and had so many people on its payroll that Nashville was just turned around. The streets were full of strange-looking people, of course; no local young men were around."

The winter of 1917-1918 was terribly cold. Over one period snow lay unmelted for twelve days, 18.5 inches deep. In December of 1917 the low temperature was minus 6; on the morning of January 12, 1918, minus 17. This made the effect of the worldwide influenza pandemic worse. Stanley Horn recalled that hundreds of workers at the powder plant died; "big truckloads came to Nashville undertakers every day. I'd look out the window of my office and see 'em go by, a harrowing sight." In

October of 1917 one funeral director buried 117 persons—ten on one day. A Nashville soldier wrote from training camp that the men had to "march three feet apart; cover our mouth and nose with a handkerchief when you cough or sneeze."

A Nashville soldier, Pvt. Glenn Gladhill, wrote home about the last months of the war: "All the pep we got from America makes us twice as strong, and gave us just what it took to finish the game. The pivotal time of the war was when we stopped the Germans at Chateau Thierry, for after that they continued to lose from one front to the next. The Americans didn't prove the cowards they expected and their soldiers learned a great deal more then than the Kaiser was able to belie. The St. Mihiel was just a sample of what we could do when we wanted to as we later showed them in the Argonne."

To Catch the Kaiser

In December of 1918 while encamped at Tuntingen, Luxemburg, the men and officers of the 114th Field Artillery found themselves more comfortably quartered than they had been in many months, and also with time on their hands. Col. Luke Lea of Nashville and a party composed of three other officers and four noncoms traveled to Amerongen, Holland, to interview Kaiser Wilhelm. It was all quite regular, Colonel Lea insisted; he had the permission of General Spalding to make the trip and passports signed by Queen Wilhelmina. His real intent was to take the Kaiser into custody and bring him to France where he could be tried for war crimes. They arrived at the castle of Count Bentinck and were admitted. Told of their arrival the Kaiser declined to see them unless they could show credentials stating that they were official representatives of the American government. Meanwhile the count, suspecting for some reason that an attempt was to be made to abduct his imperial guest, doubled the guard around the castle. Colonel Lea withdrew gracefully, and later a full investigation was conducted which found that no regulations had been violated! However the Kaiser for several months refused to leave the castle unless he was with an armed guard.

To Honor Strength and Valor

In 1919 funds totaling $1 million were made available by state, county, and city governments for the erection of a suitable building to honor 3400 Tennesseans who had died in the war. A location on Capitol Boulevard, between Union and Cedar streets, was chosen. The building was completed in 1925. It is a three-storey limestone structure, somewhat resembling a Greek temple but in neo-Classic style, designed by McKim, Mead & White (Edward Daugherty was the firm's Nashville associate). The main entrance, from what is now the Legislative Plaza but which was then called Victory Park, is into a wide central court, open at the top, between the two main sections. This court is reached from the east by wide stone steps leading to a Doric portico. There are large fluted columns. In the center of the court there stands a bronze statue of a young man in heroic pose symbolizing the strength and valor of soldiers. The statue is by Belle Kinney of Nashville and her Austrian husband Leopold Scholz. There are bronze tablets on the western side of the court, bearing the names of the war dead. The north hall contained state offices; the south an auditorium seating 2200. In the basement for many years was located the Tennessee State Museum, which placed major emphasis on artifacts and mementoes of the wars in which Tennesseans had fought.

The auditorium became the focus of cultural life: in it performed not only the new Nashville Symphony but also many renowned artists such as Vladimir Horowitz and Robert Merrill, brought by such local organizations as Community Concerts. Here too the Grand Ole Opry was staged until it was moved to the Ryman; here speakers such as Adlai Stevenson addressed audiences that filled the hall to its capacity.

"Where Every Prospect Pleases"

From the end of the war until the faint distant thunder of economic trouble began to be heard, Nashville was looked on by many as Eden. True, the poor were there, often living in squalor. True, the black community was segregated. But whatever else may be said of the Howse regime it always worked to better the lot of the people; the rich could take care of themselves, and did, in beautiful, fashionable homes, with expensive automobiles, trips abroad, fine clothes, and the delicious cuisine for which the Central South had become famous. The professional and mercantile class enjoyed a higher standard of living: the suburbs were green and pleasant. Life was not a rat race, although in "Fire On Belmont Street," perhaps his best poem, Donald Davidson warned of the perils of materialism. By 1925 Davidson County had turned the corner of the century, had set its feet on the way out of post-Confederate backwaters, and knew where it wanted to go.

Opry Town

Davidson County's position as the trading center for the counties to its east, the valleys of the Cumberland, Stone's, Caney Fork, and Obed rivers, the Cumberland Plateau as far east as Mayland, as far south as Tracy City, as far north as Monticello, Eddyville, and even Somerset, Kentucky, was suddenly immensely augmented by the tremendous force of radio. No longer a toy for young boys to tinker with in the shed, radio, emancipated from ponderous and clumsy batteries, entered the home in the middle 1920s.

Nashville was early into the electronic game. WTNT, "The Dynamite of Dixie," Luke Lea's broadcasting station, in 1929 shared air time with WDAD, Dad's Tire Store on Broad. Life and Casualty Insurance Company was quick to see how insurance could be sold by a salesman on whom no door could slam and established WLAC. But above all, there was WSM—"We Shield Millions"—the National Life and Accident Insurance Company, the "Shield" company, one of the county's major employers. And WSM would be given what the Federal Communications Commission called "a clear channel," so it could reach thousands of farm homes without interference from other transmitters, giving the rural audience the same message their city cousins enjoyed. If television would be, thirty years later, a revolution, radio was an earthquake.

The Grand Ole Opry from 1925, when it began, until 1941, when its character began to change, was the dominant voice of rural Tennessee culture in America. It was pure corn, overalls, fruit jars, possum, and bird dogs. The Texas honky-tonk swing, rhinestones, and electronics would come, each in turn, later. But from the start it was show business. From 1925 the show has never missed a Saturday night broadcast. WSM carried no network programs on Saturday night.

In a sense Sidney Johnson Harkreader was the first full-time musician on the Saturday night show. Others had regular work of other kinds, but the fiddle was Sid's life. He was not only there when George D. Hay, "The Solemn Old Judge,"named the country music broadcast the Grand Ole Opry but Fiddlin' Sid played the first tune after Dr. Walter Damrosch's program of classical music on NBC had ended and the air was given back to the local station. "You've heard grand opera," observed Hay, "now let's hear Grand Ole Opry!" Fiddlin' Sid, Uncle Dave Macon, and Dr. Humphrey Bate and his Hawaiian orchestra played on the first remote control broadcast from WSM. This was no hole-in-the-wall personal appearance, but a performance before 6000 people sponsored by the Nashville Policemen's Benefit Association and held in what has come to be called "the mother church of country music," Ryman Auditorium. This program was on November 6, 1925, and was advertised as "An Evening With WSM," featuring "these artists and musicians in person that you listen to over your radio every evening." The advertisement in the newspapers urged: "Hear Uncle Dave and Fiddlin' Sid on the banjo and guitar." The two had recorded for Aeolian Vocalion Record Company in New York City on July 10, 1924, and discographers say that it is almost certain they were the first from Tennessee to record traditional country music. "Uncle Jimmy " Thompson was 77 when Hay asked him to play on the radio and within a month, he was known all over the country. That more or less impromptu show from the studio was the beginning of regular country music programming on WSM. The first tune "Uncle Jimmy"played was "The Tennessee Wagoner,"as best anyone can now remember. According to the best-known anecdote,

Hay suggested after an hour that the old man might be getting tired. Thompson replied, "An hour? Fiddlesticks! A man can't get warmed up in an hour. I just won an eight-day fiddling contest down in Dallas and here's my blue ribbon to prove it. This program's got to be longer." Deford Bailey, harmonica player deluxe, also has a claim to being the first to play on the Opry, and he lasted on the show until the 1940s, longer than either Thompson, whose regular appearances ceased after mid-1927, or Harkreader. Apparently the name "Grand Ole Opry" was given in January of 1926, although it did not appear in published radio programs until December of 1927.

The Fugitives Speak Out

Nashville's voice to the nation was not only expressed by radio. A little magazine, produced by a group of Vanderbilt University students and teachers between 1922 and 1925, changed the course of American poetry. *The Fugitive* was influential far beyond its expectations.

John Crowe Ransom, years later looking back on a distinguished career, said: "It was all something of an accident, really. We were brought together in a particular time and place that favored the kind of thing we were going to do, to do it actually without knowing what we were going to do; without knowing what it was that we intended to do or, even, that we intended to do it."

The group of young men would gather of evenings in a house on Whitland Avenue, the home of a Nashville merchant. They read poetry, poems that they had written, and they listened and severely criticized, and they pondered the esoteric philosophizing and speculative inquiries of Sidney Mttron Hirsch.

This had actually had its beginnings in 1914 when Donald Davidson enrolled in Ransom's Shakespeare course. Other gifted teachers on the English faculty were Edwin Mims, the chairman, and Walter Clyde Curry. With Davidson in their classes were other bright young men. Ransom, Davidson, Curry, William Yandell Elliott, Stanley Johnson, and Alec Brock Stevenson were drawn into discussions in a congenial group that

The James M. Frank house on Whitland Avenue was the regular meeting place of the Fugitives from 1920 to 1928. These young students became one of the most influential groups of poets and critics of the twentieth century.

met in the Hirsch apartment near the campus. Interrupted by the war the meetings resumed at the home of James M. Frank (Hirsch's brother-in-law) with poetry the center of the group's interest.

These, and Merrill Moore, son of John Trotwood Moore, writer and editor; Allen Tate; and eventually Robert Penn Warren; Laura Riding, wife of a Midwestern professor; Ridley and Jesse Wills; William Frierson; Alfred Starr; and Andrew Lytle founded the little magazine, or joined the group, or contributed to it. There were other contributors, some already well known, such as Witter Bynner or Hart Crane; but no one, then or now, considered them Fugitive poets. *The Fugitive* was published from April 1922 to December 1925; Jacques Back had been a successful business manager: its ceasing to publish was not caused by insolvency.

In 1928, national recognition followed the publication of *Fugitives: An Anthology*, but by then literary fame had come to many of the group. Five of them had turned their attention to public affairs: Tate, Davidson, Ransom, Warren, and Lytle, with others of the Vanderbilt community—Lyle Lanier, Frank Owsley, H. C. Nixon—conceived a symposium advocating the Agrarian ideal (or "the southern way of life") as a remedy for the increasingly visible ills of finance capitalism and the industrial ethos. In 1930 the symposium, *I'll Take My Stand*, containing a statement of principles, written by Ransom, and essays by these five Fugitives and Lanier, Owsley, Nixon, John Donald Wade, Henry Blue Kline, John Gould Fletcher (the Imagist poet), and Stark Young (the New York theater critic), appeared. It was a challenging book whose central thrust was completely misunderstood. That it has survived as a work of influence is due, according to the scholar Louis Rubin, who wrote the preface to a later edition, to the fact that the subject of the symposium was not topical but universal: Man, "in his zeal for the benefits of modern scientific civilization...was placing so high a value on material gain that he ignored his own spiritual welfare and his moral obligations to society."

Six years later a second symposium, *Who Owns America?* edited by Tate and historian Herbert Agar, included essays by the five Fugitives, three of the other Agrarians, and thirteen additional contributors recruited by Tate and Agar (T. S. Eliot, Sinclair Lewis, and Dorothy Thompson were also invited and accepted but did not complete their contributions). In 1938 Davidson alone published *The Attack on Leviathan*, a final work of social protest. Ransom had been lost to Vanderbilt and Nashville in 1937 when the university declined to meet an offer by Kenyon College, to the dissatisfaction of many of Ransom's friends but to the probable advancement of Ransom's career as a literary critic: he founded *The Kenyon Review*, one of the most influential voices of the New Criticism.

The distinguished poet, Randall Jarrell, was as a teen-aged boy the model for the sculpture of Ganymede, cup-bearer of the gods *(fifth figure from left)*, on the west pediment of the Parthenon.

Cupbearer to the Gods

One of the younger generation of poets influenced by the Fugitives, Randall Jarrell, student of Ransom and one of the few American poets of the period to write lasting poems about World War II, is memorialized in a unique way. As a 14-year-old Nashville boy he was the model for the figure of Ganymede, cupbearer to the Olympians who are sculptured on the western pediment of the Parthenon. This replica in concrete of the classical temple which stands on the Acropolis of Athens was completed in 1931. First erected for the Tennessee Centennial of 1897, it was reproduced in more durable materials by Hart, Freeland, and Roberts as a permanent part of the city's cultural monuments. The Doric columns of the peristyle are more than six feet in diameter and the double bronze doors weigh 15 tons. The decorations of the Doric frieze are by George J. Zolnay; the

Amqui Railway Station, formerly Edgefield Junction on the Nashville, Chattanooga & St. Louis Railway near Madison, where tracks to Louisville and St. Louis went their separate ways. (sketched by Michael Birdwell from a photograph)

54 statues are by Belle Kinney and Leopold Scholz. A statue of Pallas Athene is being completed (1988) and will be erected inside the great court.

Out to the Suburbs

Although there had been "additions" to the city, Davidson County's development had followed the traditional pattern of villages at the crossroads—a store, a church, a schoolhouse, a post office. There had been New Town (West Nashville) and South Nashville, Edgefield too. Belle Meade's deer park was divided. Tusculum, Antioch, Couchville, and Goodlettsville were towns in their own right. The streetcar lines had been an incentive for having the advantages of both rural and urban living.

But it was Bluefields that was the county's first true subdivision of the twentieth century. A. F. and R. D. Stanford went from

Tennessee to Oklahoma, made money, and returned to Tennessee in 1918. Donelson (which has been known by many names, including Spring Place, Slip-up, and McWhirtersville, according to regional historian Leona Taylor Aiken) was confined by the McGavock properties, the McMurrays' land, and the Hoggatts' Clover Bottom Farms. Buying Clover Bottom, the Stanfords started residential and business development. Robert Donnell Stanford, Sr., built a row of fine houses along Lebanon Road across from Clover Bottom mansion. Then came business buildings in Donelson. In 1929, to the accompaniment of full-page newspaper promotional advertising, a city real estate company opened a subdivision named Bluefields on the northern part of the McMurray land. When the company ran into difficulties the Stanfords took over. The original development included 111 lots and was served by a new eight-inch water line brought out from the city. Viewed by travelers from the Donelson overpass, the first houses were like a dream of the future, as indeed the development proved to be.

The Banks Tumble Down

There has been for many years a symbiotic relationship between banking and politics—Andrew Jackson's struggle with the Bank of the United States was by no means the first example. In Davidson County in the 1930s the connection was to have painful consequences. In October of 1929 the stock market crashed, but this had little effect in Davidson County, Tennessee. It was in November of 1930 that the storm hit Caldwell & Company, the Bank of Tennessee, the American National, the Fourth and First National, and Tennessee Hermitage National. The first two failed; the second and third merged; the last was taken over by the Commerce Union Bank. Although that bank and the Broadway National, American National, and Third National came through the crisis, deposits in these banks fell from $107 million in September of 1930 to $64,250,000 two years later. It was the fall of Caldwell & Company that was the most spectacular because of the ramifications. Luke Lea, former U.S. Senator and newspaper publisher, and banker Rogers Caldwell were controlling partners. Early in 1930 the value of the firm's stock and property began to decline sharply; a merger with Banco Kentucky of Louisville was arranged. The transaction required several risky financial moves that eventually led to receivership for the Bank of Tennessee. In the end the State of Tennessee lost $6.5 million in deposits; this led to an attempt to impeach Governor Henry Horton, who had been supported by Lea. (The storm toppled 120 banks in seven states: its effects in western North Carolina are preserved in a famous novel by Ashevillian Thomas Wolfe.) And indirectly the affair enabled the Crump political organization to take control of the state government for 32 of the next 38 years.

The New Deal Comes In

In 1933 the Tennessee Valley Authority was created; in 1935 the Works Progress Administration was established. Both provided jobs; the TVA made cheap electricity possible for every home, farm, and business. In the Nashville District of WPA, Col. Harry S. Berry was director. He made possible the financing of farm-to-market road projects, construction of schools, gymnasiums, parks—including the restoration of Fort Negley and improvement of Percy and Edwin Warner parks—and construction of the airport that bears his name (BNA—the abbreviation for the field—is "Berry, NAshville"). The Public Works Administration built a new city market. On August 10, 1936, Mayor Hilary E. Howse spoke at the dedication of the new post office, a model of Art Deco architecture.

President Franklin D. Roosevelt visited Nashville with Mrs. Roosevelt in 1934. People lined the streets: the symbol of hope for the common man, FDR did not come as a guest of prominent persons in elegant mansions, and his visit to the Hermitage signaled the link the New Deal sought with Jacksonian democracy. Nine of the fourteen presidents since Lincoln had visited the city but none had come since Taft (although while president of Princeton, Dr. Woodrow Wilson had spoken in Nashville).

The great snow of February 1929 reached the axles of this Model T Ford and eventually 15 inches.

Weather, Hot and Cold, Wet and Dry

In memory few things stand out as vividly as the weather. A tornado swept through the village of Una in 1917, the frigid winter of 1917–18 marked that decade. Twice rainy winters had caused the Cumberland River to come out of its banks: in late December 1926 and early January 1927, there was a total of 11.49 inches of rain and both Stone's and the Cumberland rivers overflowed. On Christmas Day 1926 more than 5000 people were forced to leave their homes. The water at one point was three miles wide. Again in January 1937 there was a major flood; the river crested at 53.8 feet (56.15 ten years before) and much of the area next to the river was under water. That was the time of the dreadful Louisville flood: Station WSM stayed on the air around the clock helping the Kentuckians with a constant, desperate flow of emergency messages: "Send a boat…"

East Nashville, devastated by fire in 1916, was struck by a tornado on March 14, 1933. The funnel first touched a corner of the Public Square, leaped the river, and destroyed houses between the railroad and Woodland Street, and then on Porter Road and Inglewood. Ten persons were killed, over 1500 houses destroyed.

And the winter of 1940 cannot be forgotten (although 1963 and 1985 were as frigid) because on January 26, 1940, the river at Nashville froze so hard any number of people could walk across. It had been so when James Robertson's party arrived; it had been frozen in the 1890s; but because of the dams and reservoirs it would not ever be so again. As long as that generation lived they would remember and tell their grandchildren.

Jack Norman's Nashville

In a column in *The Nashville Banner* in the 1980s lawyer Jack Norman reminisced, usually beginning, "Do You Remember?" He might have remembered these...

Joe Hatcher, Red O'Donnell, Bowser Chest, Blinkey Horn, the Golden Gloves, the Hippodrome, Nick Gulas, Chief Chewacki, Lasses and Honey, Skeets Mayo, names sharp in memory but fading, fading.

Once Albert Bell, age 100, recalled a circus that performed in the 1840s. Ten thousand people had crowded to see it. "Of all that vast concourse," he said, mournfully, "only she and I were left alive to remember, and now she is gone and only I am left."

"He hit it on top of the ice house!" Francis Craig and "Red Rose." Pen Pick-Ups by Parrish. Moon River, David Cobb, Charley Roberts, the Old Night Owl, the Hermitage, the Andrew Jackson, and the Sam Davis. Sulphur Dell, Flo Fleming, Lance Richbourg, Phil Weintraub, the Vols of 1934, little David Scobey and the Bisons of 1940. Do you remember June 1941 when Tommy Tatum hit three home runs over the left field fence? Or back in 1932 when Stan Keyes hit one over the flagpole in center field? And:

The East Eagles, the DuPont Bulldogs, the Donelson Dons, the Burk Terrors. Nabrico, Loew's Vendome, the Paramount, the Fifth Avenue, the Knickerbocker, the Princess, Loew's. If you called it the Vendome, you had to have been born before 1920.

Do you remember when *Gone With the Wind* first showed in Nashville? January 1940, and there were reserved seats. On that cold night did you stand in that long line along Church Street, around the corner and down the alley, waiting for the doors to open? And do you remember the unbelievable beauty of that first scene when it was "quittin' time at Tara"?

Do you remember Marian Ellis, Dorothy Ann Distlehurst,

the Still kidnapping? Did your *Banner* boy drop your afternoon paper flat on the front walk as he rode by on his bicycle on the sidewalk, or did he fold it and pitch it? Did you read Tailspin Tommy, Dan Dunn, Secret Agent X-9, Buck Rogers, Krazy Kat, Barney Google, Gasoline Alley, Little Orphan Annie, Steve Canyon (but then it was called "Terry and the Pirates")? Did you listen to Vic and Sade, Clara, Lou, and Em, Pepper Young's Family, Eddie Cantor, Shep Fields and his Rippling Rhythm with a brash young comic named Bob Hope? Did you follow One Man's Family, or hear the Met on Saturday afternoons, or the Philharmonic on Sundays?

Did you ever stop in at Dean's Tasty-Toasty across from the old Vanderbilt dental school in South Nashville? (Dean Wilkinson, who played football for Harvard before he played for Hume-Fogg!)

Did you eat at The Owl, or see Doc Godwin at the pharmacy or at Dudley Field every game? Do you remember Smokey Joe in the *Tennessean* Cartoons, or Mrs. Naff, or Signor de Luca, or Madame Galli-Curci, or Fritz Leiber in *The Merchant of Venice*? ("Study Shakespeare, young gentlemen, you never know when you might quote him to good effect to a jury!") Did you read about Walter Liggett, Abby Arnett, Gus Kiger, or Albert Vaughan? Did you go into Candyland, Zibart's, Mills', the Satsuma Tea Room, the B. & W., Shacklett's or Walgreen's at the entrance to the Arcade? Did your parents take you into Burk's for your first big boy's suit? Or did you go into Dury's or Steiff's, with that jewelers' smell, or to the old Phillips and Buttorff store that had those tremendously high ceilings? Did you know Albert Williams and hear him quote the jingle that Governor Roberts could not duck?

Sunday, December 7, 1941, marked the end of a world.

By the Stove at Harvey's

In 1941 a new day came to downtown Nashville and to Middle Tennessee merchandising. Fred Harvey, who had learned the department store business in Chicago, bought Lebeck Broth-

Candyland, on Church Street, was the meeting place for
three generations of shoppers.

ers, an old-line Nashville store with desirable Church Street
frontage, and made showmanship pay. He renamed the store
Harvey's, adopted the slogan "The Store That Never Knows
Completion," acquired some used merry-go-round horses from
a defunct carnival, had them repainted and installed as a kind
of trademark, eventually expanded into adjoining buildings,
and installed the first escalators in Middle Tennessee. Hiring experienced window dressers from larger cities, he made his
Christmas windows the talk of the town, sponsored an elaborate
Christmas display at Centennial Park every holiday season, and
kept the pot boiling generally. "Meet me by the stove at Harvey's
(referring to an old-fashioned—and nonfunctioning—black
potbellied stove near the west entrance) became a byword with
shoppers. His competitors, principally nearby department
stores like Cain-Sloan and Castner-Knott, remained competitive

by hustling but for twenty years it was Fred Harvey's that set the pace. And Harvey came to Nashville because of Ed Potter.

In 1916, Edward Potter, Jr., organized a new bank in Nashville, with the approval of his father, A. E. Potter of the Broadway National Bank, where young Potter was employed. The German American Bank was located near the Public Square. The word "German" at that time signified stability and financial solidity and was attractive to Davidson County's prosperous German-American community. The war caused a change of name: first to the Farmers and Merchants, then later to Commerce Union. In 1941 Lebeck Brothers store, which owed the bank a considerable sum, filed a petition in bankruptcy, asking reorganization. Commerce Union was awarded ownership of the lease on the Church Street building. Later a broker informed Potter that the manager of the basement store of Marshall Field & Company in Chicago, a man named Fred Harvey, might take over the store. Talking face to face with Harvey, as he preferred to do, Potter asked: "How much of your own capital are you willing to invest?" Harvey gave just the right answer: "Everything I have in the world—$65,000." Ed Potter had brought a merchandising genius to Nashville.

While the Storm Clouds Gather

A Nashville newspaperman, Herman Eskew, thought that the absolute peak of American civilization before the Second World War was a 1941 maroon Ford V-8. Premonitions aside, the summer and fall of that year were pretty good: defense contracts meant more employment, the cost of living was reasonable, there were good things to buy in the stores, and the weather was nice. Hitler had invaded Russia and knowledgeable folk said this meant Germany's eventual defeat. At least he wouldn't have time to think about invading England or taking Egypt or meddling with America. Japan? Our fleet controlled the Pacific, didn't it?

In 1938 the WPA had built an eighteen-jump three-mile course in Percy Warner Park, and in May of 1941 the first running of the Iroquois Steeplechase took place, a pleasant event which has survived.

The Ryman Auditorium, for decades the home of the Grand Ole Opry.

The Ryman Auditorium had become a center of the arts in Nashville. Thomas G. Ryman was a riverboat captain in the 1880s; Sam Jones of Georgia was a traveling revival preacher whose meetings drew great crowds. Hearing Jones in 1885, Ryman underwent a religious conversion and decided to build an auditorium for meetings by Jones and other preachers. Hugh Thompson of Nashville was the architect; its imposing facade faced North Summer Street. Called the Union Gospel Tabernacle, the building was used for other large public assemblies, including a Confederate reunion, for which a balcony, still called the Confederate Gallery, was installed. The first meeting was held by Jones in 1890, although the building had not been finished. By 1894 the role of Town Hall formerly filled by the Hall of the House of Representatives had been taken over by what came to be known as Ryman Auditorium after the captain's death in 1904. Almost every celebrity of politics, theater, and music played the Ryman during the next sixty years. Its grande dame from 1910 to 1959 was the legendary Mrs. L. C. Naff. But in the late autumn of 1941 the Ryman met its true destiny. The Grand Ole Opry moved in. Minnie Pearl (Mrs. Henry Cannon) is the best source, with Roy Acuff, for events of those carefree days. She had joined the show in her role as a country girl from Grinder's Switch in November of 1940 (for $10), performing at the War Memorial building. She was on the road when the increasing crowds caused the show to move. When she returned and was put into the Prince Albert NBC segment of the radio show with Whitey Ford, the Duke of Paducah, as another comic and Acuff as master of ceremonies, the Opry began to move into the format that it followed for another quarter century. It was in 1941 that something else happened to forever change the show: Bob Wills did a guest spot wearing an all-white suit and a white cowboy hat: no more bib overalls for the musicians.

The War Years

On December 7, 1941, as it did to all the nation, war came to Davidson County. It was a pleasant, sunny December Sunday. Home from church, their dinner eaten, the Sunday newspaper divided among the family, the radio turned on (every Sunday afternoon WSM broadcast the New York Philharmonic), they found real the apprehensions that had been felt with increasing force since the blitzkrieg overran the Low Countries and France in 1940, but in an unexpected way. The sudden interruption— "Japanese planes have bombed Pearl Harbor"—should not have come as a surprise. The afternoon newspaper the day before had carried the front page headline: "Civilians Warned to Leave Manila." But from every Davidson County home went the question: "Have you heard? Have you heard?"

Nashville mobilized. For nearly four years the city was a focus of military activity: as a transportation center; as the railhead for the gigantic Tennessee Maneuvers of Second Army; as the nearest city to the 20th Ferrying Group headquarters at Seward Air

Force Base in Smyrna, to Fort Campbell, and to the Air Force Classification Center on Thompson Lane.

The Aviation Manufacturing Company built the first defense plant, adjoining Berry Field; it was bought by Vultee Aircraft Inc. in 1940 to produce the Vultee Vengeance, a dive bomber which never lived up to its expected potential although it saw action with the British Royal Air Force and the Indian Air Force in Burma and India. Vultee also produced Lockheed P-38 Lightning fighters. In 1942 the Nashville Bridge Company began to build minesweepers for the Navy.

In 1942 a Davidson County officer, Lt. Gen. Frank W. Andrews, was named commander of U.S. Army Ground Forces in Europe. He was killed in an aircraft crash in Iceland in May of 1943.

Also in 1942 the Army Air Force established on Thompson Lane a large Classification Center which processed air recruits after their initial indoctrination and determined their future training as pilots, navigators, or bombardiers. Later, when this need slackened, the center became a convalescent hospital. Thayer General Hospital, constructed on White Bridge Road, was for more serious cases, and later became a Veterans Administration Hospital.

In 1943, while on a training flight in Texas, the plane flown by Cornelia Fort, a pilot for the WASPS, crashed. She was killed, the first woman pilot to die in active service in the United States. She was 23. Cornelia Fort Airport is named in her honor.

The WASPS—Women's Army Service Pilots—were promised full military status with all benefits accruing to members of the Armed Forces. In a singular breach of faith, the Department of Defense reneged on this promise. Nashville provided another WASP pilot—Jennie Lou Gower, member of one of Nashville's pioneer families. She learned to fly in the Civilian Pilot Training Program while in college, joined the service after America entered the war and flew air transport for thousands of miles and survived to reside in California for many years, until her death in 1986.

Second Army Maneuvers

In the autumn of 1942 a decision was made to resume field maneuvers in Middle Tennessee. Large scale war games had been conducted in an area around Camp Forrest, near Tullahoma, the previous summer, and General George S. Patton had perfected the armored tactics that were to bring him fame and his divisions victory in Europe. Between the wars Erwin Rommel, as a young military attache, had visited Nashville and Middle Tennessee, following the cavalry campaigns of Confederate General Nathan Bedford Forrest, making them a pattern for the use of tank units as cavalry. Now the Army, perceiving in the Cumberland River and the hilly country to the south and north a similarity to the Rhine and western Europe, decided to send divisions into the state for their last preparation before actual combat.

Lebanon was chosen as headquarters and Nashville as the principal railhead. Over the hills and valleys of 21 counties the blue army and the red army engaged in weekly problems, divisions being moved in and out by a calendar of phases, each lasting about four weeks. Nashville was London, or Antwerp, or Cherbourg, without the bombing. The first and second problems usually took place east of Davidson County, but the third in each phase would poise attacking blue troops around Donelson and Couchville. This force would advance to the east toward hilly terrain. In at least one instance a problem involved the defense of Berry Field against blue airborne troops (defenders were always red).

Maneuvers paused at noon on Thursday afternoon, or at noon Friday, when a light plane would fly over the mock battle lines, sounding a siren. Then thousands of soldiers (and in the months between September 1942 and the last problem in March 1944 over one million soldiers would pass through the Tennessee Maneuver Area) would pour into Nashville and the county seat towns around, seeking recreation. Facilities were limited, in spite of the best efforts of the USO and the American Red Cross; movie theaters were packed, cafes were packed, drug store soda

Troops of Second Army held full scale maneuvers in Davidson and other Middle Tennessee counties from 1941 to 1944 to prepare for battle in Europe. This scene is near Couchville. (photo by U.S. Army)

fountains were forced to shut down twice a day for clean-up. Each PX was strained to the limit. Hundreds roamed the sidewalks looking for something of interest. Churches opened their doors and set up lounges, schools opened their gyms for weekend dances. The Grand Ole Opry had never drawn such crowds, nor had Nashville had such an experience since 1865.

At Remagen Bridge

On March 7, 1945, the city of Cologne was in Allied hands. A task force of the Ninth Armored Division in which Lt. Hugh Mott of Nashville was an officer moved up to the west bank of the Rhine to the little town of Remagen. The railroad bridge across the river was intact. The German lieutenant assigned to the demolition job had boasted in a cafe that the bridge would go up at 4 o'clock. It was 3:50 P.M. The Americans, led by Mott, scrambled onto the bridge snatching up wires and explosives. When the charges were set off, there were two small blasts. The bridge did not fall. The Americans were over the Rhine. The whole strategic plan of both Allies and Germans had to be altered quickly. The bold charge of that platoon had altered the course of the war. And in the Tennessee maneuvers, one problem never presented was how to capture a bridge.

The False Armistice

A mystery never solved originated in Nashville on August 12, 1945. The United Press had moved on its wires: "The President has just announced that Japan has just accepted the surrender terms of the Allies." Two minutes later, but not soon enough to stop many radio stations from putting the erroneous "flash" on air, a "kill" message went out. A confidential investigation followed. Its results were inconclusive. However, it was determined that the bulletin came over the southern wire, which was sending news at the time (8:35 P.M.); that only Memphis and Nashville could have originated the message; and that Nashville was the most probable source. The only United Press sending machine in Davidson County was in the bureau offices on the twelfth floor of the Third National Bank Building, adjoining the studios of

Radio Station WLAC. On Sunday nights the office manager, Alice Loss, did not work. The only persons in the UP office were Donald Taylor, radio news editor of WLAC, and his wife. Taylor, an experienced wire service reporter, told investigators that there was no way the message could have come from that office because it came in on the radio wire while he was there. And the wording of the message was not that prescribed for a "flash," which according to style instructions has no articles, verb auxiliaries, or qualifications. An experienced operator would have said: "President Announces Japan Accepts Surrender Terms." The mystery was never solved. Japan's surrender was announced two days later, at 6 P.M., Tuesday, August 14, Central War Time. The sale of beer was stopped in Davidson County for 24 hours.

Soon afterward Colonel Jack DeWitt of Nashville (head of WSM) was the first person to make radar contact with the moon. This scientific accomplishment, intended simply as research in communications technology, has led to most of the developments in twentieth century space science. The little blip returning after a few seconds was the equivalent of the beeps heard a half century earlier from Marconi's tiny transmitter.

Renewal

Over 36,000 Davidson County men and women had seen service; 734 died.

After the dislocations of war and the deterioration of time, the key word from 1945 to 1951 was renewal. Most obvious, after the needs of public utilities, was the area around the State Capitol. In 1949 the Capitol Hill redevelopment project began, one of the first federal urban renewal projects in the nation. First to go were the shacks and slums along Jo Johnston and Gay streets, 96 acres being cleared to make room for the James Robertson Parkway. Not until 1957 did the project near completion. In 1960, with the new landscaping of the Capitol grounds, the extensive renovation and repair of the building itself was finished. Surrounding it were a new municipal auditorium, a new state library and archives building, and office buildings, public and private, including the 31-storey National Life Center.

Schools

Tennessee Agricultural & Industrial College, established in 1909 by act of the General Assembly as a normal school and opened for classes in 1912, was given university status in 1951. It had had various definitions of role and scope over the years but had attained full Land Grant University recognition before 1979 when the U.S. District Court in response to litigation ordered the University of Tennessee at Nashville to be merged with it. After the merger, the campus consisted of the 150-acre main site, the modern facility at Charlotte and McLemore which had housed the predominantly evening classes of U-T Nashville, and 320 acres of farm land. Within the university there are eight schools. Hopes that a School of Veterinary Medicine might be added were disappointed when this was awarded the University of Tennessee at Knoxville.

In 1953 it was conceded among educators that the school systems of Nashville and Davidson County were the best in the state. There were then 24 schools in the athletic conference called the Nashville Interscholastic League (NIL). Of these, three were located outside the county; three, Montgomery Bell Academy, Father Ryan, and Harpeth Hall, were private schools. The eighteen public schools were West, East, North, Cohn, Hume-Fogg, Isaac Litton, Donelson, DuPont, Hillsboro, Central, Madison, Cumberland, Joelton, Antioch, Howard, Bellevue, Goodlettsville, and Tennessee Industrial School (soon to become Tennessee Preparatory School). In addition there were the predominantly black schools: Pearl, Haynes, and Cameron. In 20 years the movement toward large comprehensive high schools would eliminate a dozen of these, including some that were considered among the most effective teaching institutions in Tennessee.

The first large public high school in the county, Hume-Fogg stands at the corner of Eighth and Broad.

A Musical Interlude

Attention should be paid to what may have been the liveliest musical group in the county during the late 1940s: El Chico! Playing for parties (and any other occasion opportunity offered) Mrs. Weaver Harris (whose nickname was generally applied to the entire group) led with her fiddle through a repertoire of lively numbers, including "Listen to the Mockingbird." Centered on the Murfreesboro Road, but by no means confined to that neighborhood, the players were Lanier Merritt, a noted collector of Confederate memorabilia, on the banjo; Mrs. James Killebrew; Mrs. Mary Organ Elliott; Herschel Gower, Vanderbilt professor and author; Mrs. Oscar Noel (Eleanor Crawford); Mrs. Harris; Claudine Estes; Jennie Gower (Wynne), a wartime

WASP pilot; Ruth Bumpass; Paul Brown; Morton Howell; and Mrs. I. B. Dilzer. Nashville social life will never be the same.

The Great Ice Storm

For ten days in the winter of 1951 Davidson County was gripped by snow and ice, the worst in the county's history, certainly in terms of disruption of daily life. Some called it a blizzard; it was not. The event began with a chilly rain on January 30. Late in the afternoon it could be observed that the rain was freezing into ice as soon as it touched a hard surface. That night the rain became sleet and on January 31 the temperature dropped to minus 1 as snow began to mix with the sleet. Snow fell on top of the ice, tree limbs began to fall and power lines to snap, and 16,000 homes were without electricity.

On February 2 the groundhog was effectively sealed into his burrow, shadow or no shadow, and the temperature was down to minus 13 (a record at that time). Roads and streets were blocked by fallen limbs, live wires lay crackling on the ice, and the sound of electric transformers exploding could be heard in every section. When road scrapers went out to clear the snow away, the operators found solid ice six inches thick underneath. By February 4 there had been two days of brilliant sunshine and the thermometer read above freezing. The minimum reading on the next day was 27 and ice began to thaw. On February 6 it rained, melting more of the ice. Unhappily the freeze returned on February 8 bringing glazed surfaces to streets and highways, but the great storm was over.

The Winds of Political Change

Litton Hickman had been county judge since 1917. He had presided over a body whose aim often seemed to be to protect rural Davidson County from the encroachment of a sometimes disturbing urban community. Under the Tennessee Constitution of 1870, a county might be divided into as many as 25 civil districts. Each was entitled to two magistrates as members of the county quarterly court. Any district containing an incorporated town was entitled to another, elected by voters of that town, and the county seat was entitled to one more. In smaller counties this resulted in approximate proportional representation; in a county with a very large city, the representation was quite disproportionately skewed toward the rural citizens. It was not Beverly Briley's aim to alter this situation; that remained for the landmark *Baker* vs. *Carr* decision of the U.S. Supreme Court, a suit initiated by *The Nashville Tennessean* with nationwide consequences. Briley's appeal was that of an energetic, progressive young man. In 1950 he defeated Judge Hickman. In 1951 the reins of city government were handed by Thomas L. Cummings, who had succeeded Hilary Howse in 1938 and whose administration had moved the city forward through the war years, to Ben West, a young attorney. Their race had been close. West won by 55 votes. Briley and West worked closely together in planning the future development of city and county. Quietly the first discussion of consolidation of the two governments took place. It was in a talk before the Rotary Club on June 21, 1955, that Briley first made his thinking public: there must be a single consolidated metropolitan form of government; during the next sixteen months a special charter commission worked out a plan.

Growth and Growing Pains

If "renewal" had been the word for the late 1940s, "expansion" was the hallmark of 1951 to 1957.

By 1950 the student body at Vanderbilt totaled 3529. (It would double during the next 25 years.) The original campus measured 75 acres. Nashville's westward expansion, caused in some ways although not entirely by the presence of the school itself, constrained future growth. Five square blocks of residences at the western edge of the campus were acquired, not always with the cheerful willingness of the owner to sell. Then the university began to get property to the south, wiping out such residential neighborhoods as Garland Avenue, unfortunately occupied by some of Vanderbilt's most loyal supporters. By 1975 the university campus comprised 260 acres.

And in 1951 Ward-Belmont College was in trouble. In 1865 William E. Ward had established Ward's Seminary for Young La-

The Nashville Electric Service building facing the inner loop of the Interstate system resembles a Byzantine mosque of Istanbul.

dies. The Nashville Female Academy having succumbed to the dislocations of war, Ward recognized that there was an opportunity for a new institution. An alumnus of Cumberland University at Lebanon, Ward first considered locating his school there. But he opened his school in Nashville instead, to immediate success, and moved in 1866 to a building on Spruce Street.

In 1890 two ladies from Philadelphia, Ida Hood and Susan Heron, purchased the Acklen mansion, Belmont, and 15 acres of the former estate, and opened a college for women, Belmont College. During their regime many additions were made to the

house, including the part known as North Front. In 1913 Ward
Seminary and Belmont College were combined under the name
Ward-Belmont. The new school became famous throughout the
South and Southwest as a choice place to educate a young
woman. Not only were academic standards high but manners,
etiquette, and conduct were emphasized; music and art were
fields in which the carefully chosen faculty excelled. The college
operated its own country club!

But this was coming to an end. The Tennessee Baptist Convention had acquired Cumberland University in 1946 after its
Presbyterian U.S.A. sponsors had decided to place all their resources at Maryville College. The Baptists merged with their
new school Tennessee College for Women at Murfreesboro.
Both the law and college branches of the school flourished; endowment increased; an expansion program was authorized.
Meanwhile in Nashville Ward-Belmont was caught in a financial
crunch that seemed likely to cause a default on its indebtedness
to financial institutions of the city.

Late in 1950, Ward-Belmont's creditors quietly proposed a
plan to the executive committee of the Baptist Convention:
Merge with Cumberland, move the older college to Nashville,
sell its property, and become solvent again. The storm that this
caused in the spring of 1951 has largely been forgotten, but its
consequences have been far-reaching: under the leadership of
Susan Souby, the principal, the faculty of Ward-Belmont preparatory school, a profitable part of the operation, withdrew to
organize Harpeth Hall School. Alumni of Cumberland rallied
to preserve the historic school of law in its traditional setting and
reclaimed the Lebanon property. But by common sense and
good management and determination, Belmont survived as a
four-year coeducational college in the Baptist tradition, soundly
financed and with many modern buildings besides the Acklen
mansion and its additions.

Five Years of Change

Fred Harvey had done his part to move Nashville into the
swift stream of postwar expansion, but the years from 1957 to

1962 were to see the beginning of the end of downtown as it had been known for decades.

The decline of mass transit—first the streetcars, then the steadily contracting city bus routes—and increasing use of the personal automobile produced a parking crisis. There was no way to solve the problem in a Nashville of narrow downtown streets and space too valuable to abandon to parking lots. And in 1960 the civil rights movement entered downtown Nashville, variety store lunch counters, specifically.

Early that year hundreds of black Nashvillians began a campaign of "sit-ins" at McClellan's, Woolworth's, and Walgreen's on Fifth Avenue North. That was a snowy winter but a heavy snow on February 13 did not stop a march of over a hundred persons, mostly Fisk and TSU students, into downtown. By the end of the week there were sit-ins in five stores by three hundred persons. After stormy times reason prevailed and on May 10 the color bar was abandoned at almost all downtown eating places. It must be recognized that the three months of demonstration and protest caused many women shoppers, particularly the middle-aged and elderly, to change the shopping habits of a lifetime. Indeed, emotionally and resentfully Davidson County was still segregated.

The School Doors Open

In 1954 the United States Supreme Court reversed *Plessy* vs. *Ferguson*. To the astonishment of unreconstructed Tennesseans who had hated Harry Truman and voted Republican in 1952 because of opposition to the civil rights bills, the Eisenhower administration put the weight of the federal government behind desegregation. Racial discrimination in assigning students to public schools was outlawed; "separate but equal" was no longer the law of the land. George Peabody College had admitted black students in 1953; Vanderbilt soon followed suit. In September of 1955, A. Z. Kelley, a black resident of East Nashville, decided that his son Robert ought to be admitted to East High School, within walking distance of their home, rather than ride a bus to Pearl High School, admittedly an excellent school but a long way across town. The class action lawsuit asked for the desegregation of Nashville schools. After legal sparring the board of education agreed to desegregate one grade a year. In September of 1957 the first black children entered Caldwell School. The year before the city public parks, golf courses, and pools were desegregated. A curious intruder was John Kasper, friend of the poet, Ezra Pound, and holder of views closely resembling Fascism. That fall he first came to Nashville to lead protests against desegregation of the first grade in public schools, and to make inflammatory speeches, including one in a Vanderbilt dormitory.

Gold for the Tigerbelles

Wilma Rudolph was her name and she made the name of Tigerbelle famous around the world. Coach Ed Temple was Tennessee State's women's track and field coach. His methods were thorough and inspiring. Since 1956 Temple has sent 32 track competitors into the Olympic games. They have won eleven gold medals, five silver, and four bronze medals for the United States (actually, for themselves; Olympic competition is among individuals, not nations). Temple was coach of the American women's teams in 1960 and 1964 and at Rome in 1960 Rudolph, of Clarksville, won three of the gold medals. Another successful coach whose graduates went on to professional success was John Merritt, football coach at Tennessee State.

The County Outside the City

In their books, William Waller, Don H. Doyle, and Jack Norman, Sr., recall some picturesque neighborhood names. Some of these are Cab Hollow (many residents came originally from DeKalb County), Crappy Chute, Black Bottom, Varmint Town, Slowey's Corner, Billy Goat Hill, Oklahoma, Hell's Half-Acre, Mile Pond, Melrose, Flat Rock, Woodbine, Boscobel, Sulphur Dell, and Bosley Spring. But these were all sections of the city. The county's villages had a life and a history of their own. For example, there were Antioch, Bellevue, Clover Bottom, Donel-

Granny White Market is nearly the last of the old country stores (another is Smith's Store at Una). Located near Radnor Lake at the corner of Otter Creek and Granny White pikes, the store began operation in 1927. In 1987 it was owned by Reese Smith, Jr., and operated by Helen and Howard Maxon.

son, Elm Crag, Goodlettsville, and McWhortersville.

Maple Trees at Antioch

Southeast of Nashville in the 1890s flourished the village of Antioch. The name remains and the rural atmosphere of nearly a century ago is preserved in two structures facing one another across Antioch Pike: the United Methodist Church, a white frame building erected in 1891 in clapboard Gothic, and the Lafayette Ezell house, similar in style with gables and a porch trimmed with wooden carving.

Here once there were birds, and squirrels, and rabbits among the maple trees that autumn turned red and gold in the evening sun and neighbors were just close enough, down the pike, and the country store and the community school were just a walk away.

The Neighborly Life in Bellevue

In 1960 Bellevue, west of the city in the Harpeth Hills, was a community of farms and single family homes and a high school. It was typical of the Davidson county towns of 1930-1959, a community of small-town charm and diversity, with pride in its individual personality, pride that was centered in the high school, visible as the center of Bellevue life to the motorist coming over the top of Nine Mile Hill.

When the high school was lost in the rush to comprehensive high schools of enormous size—and Bellevue was one of the last to go—the community knew anger. Many felt that this was robbing Bellevue, as it had robbed Donelson some years earlier, of something of value. In the late twentieth century many in Metropolitan Nashville and Davidson County believed that the neighborhood school is the cement that holds a neighborhood together like nothing else can do. But there are many things other than a school that hold a community together, given the will. There are, in this case, the Kroger supermarket, which takes the place of a public square as a place to sooner or later see everybody, the Natchez Trace restaurant, the community newspaper, *The Westview* (Doug Underwood, editor and publisher), and above all pride in the community's individual personality.

Fifty years ago there were mostly single family houses on tree-shaded lots along the main thoroughfare. Up a little valley there were family farms growing vegetables. There was a cafe; there was a tourist court. There may have been a few apartments but no condominiums. The Kroger store at the intersection of Old Hickory Boulevard and Highway 70 was rebuilt larger across the street; then it was rebuilt a second time, larger still, on a third corner of the two thoroughfares.

There was a large pasture in a good location. In 1981 it was proposed to build the Bellevue Regional Mall there. Six years later it was still a large grassy field. But there are 12 pizza restaurants. However, it is at the Natchez Trace that people hear the latest news, find out what's going on, shake hands with local candidates for public office, see familiar faces, call folks by their first names, share a cup of coffee in midmorning and afternoon.

On the Banks of Stone's River

A tract of 129 acres on the west bank of Stone's River, part of Clover Bottom Farms, was purchased from the State of Tennessee in 1972 by two businessmen, Clifford E. Hooper and Robert Baltz. They planned a residential, commercial, and office development costing $70 million. Apartment buildings would follow the shoreline; a shopping center would be circled by Andrew Jackson's old race track. Streets and sewer lines were built. But there was a flood of unprecedented depth in 1974. The project was abandoned.

Clover Bottom, a fertile piece of level land near the Hermitage, was traversed by the Hermitage turnpike and out-of-state automobile travelers in the 1930s marveled at the report that three crops of hay were gathered each year.

In 1805 that tract was developed into a commercial complex by Jackson, John Hutchings, and John Coffee: a general store, a boatyard, a racetrack, a tavern, and "a house of entertainment," as the proprietors advertised. An economic depression coupled with bad debts soon doomed the enterprise.

But as a farm the estate owned by John Hoggatt after 1797 and by his descendants for nearly a century flourished. He built the house which was acquired by Andrew Price, then by A. F. and R. D. Stanford, and is now used by faculty of Tennessee School for the Blind.

Franklin College at Elm Crag

Tolbert Fanning was a minister of the gospel, an educator, and a farmer and saw no incompatibility among these vocations. In 1840 he moved from Franklin to a farm five miles east of Nashville which he named Elm Crag. At the same time he was named editor of the periodical of the Tennessee Agricultural Society.

The farm was in the southern part of the old Civil District No. 2; at the opposite end of the district was McWhortersville (also called "McWhirtersville") where Donelson Post Office was located in a toll gate house.

Fanning's principal farming interest was in livestock breeding. He brought the finest of cattle, sheep, hogs, and horses to Elm Crag. In about 1845 he began to combine his interest in agriculture and education by establishing at Elm Crag an agricultural school for young men, with whom he himself labored in the fields, instructing them in the latest and most efficient methods. In 1843-44 he constructed buildings for a college which he named Franklin College, announcing:

> "Young men of the country, mechanics who are willing to work, blacksmiths, carriage or wagon makers, saddlers, carpenters, cabinet makers, printers, or plowboys can be educated at Franklin College by their labor and are earnestly invited to attend."

In 1861 because of the coming of war Fanning resigned as president; shortly the school was suspended. It was reopened in 1865 but in a short time the buildings burned and Franklin College ceased to exist.

If the Civil War left eastern Davidson County relatively unscathed, this was not true of the southern acres. For example, the Samuel Watkins farm on Hillsboro Pike four miles south of the city was in the path of Hood's advance in December of 1864. The two-storey house with its Palladian portico and four tall white columns was ransacked and robbed; the shade trees that were not felled for campfires on the bitterly cold night before the battle were mangled by cannonball and shell. His cattle were slaughtered, his horses seized for cavalry mounts, and the land scarred by trenches and the ruts of wagons and cannon wheels. Even the church building erected on the farm by the staunch old Presbyterian for the use of the Methodists of his neighborhood was destroyed.

Goodlettsville Leads the Way

The village of Goodlettsville is in a pleasant section of rolling hills and pastures planted in long-season grasses affording animals green grazing even during the winter. The soil is typical limestone-phosphate. Houses are neat and fences are well tended. In 1870 the country roads were white with the limestone which surfaced them, the streams ran clear and fresh.

All was not well: the Civil War had devastated farms as much as cities. Orchards had been chopped down, livestock slaughtered or stolen, fences burned. In 1873 there was an economic collapse that affected farmers more than any other class. Sheep raising was a dependable source of income and the price paid for a group of lambs often determined the available cash a farm family would have for the year.

It was in 1877 at Goodlettsville, situated on the border of Davidson and Sumner counties, that the first cooperative livestock marketing association in the United States was organized.

The Tennessee Agricultural Hall of Fame recognizes two Davidson County honorees: Mark Cockrill [see above, "Wool Champion of the World"] and the Goodlettsville Lamb & Wool Club.

Northern Davidson county after the severe depression of 1873 had become a center of sheep and wool production. Every farmer owned a flock of sheep and took pride in selling top grade animals when buyers came around in the spring. Some Goodlettsville farmers owned 100 sheep and would sell about that many lambs a season; others had as few as ten, but the railroad station was a busy place, as more than 2000 lambs went to the Chicago market.

Buyers would estimate weights and pay accordingly. In 1876 one skeptical farmer challenged the weight estimate and offered to take his sheep down to the scales at the depot to be sure. The buyer scoffed and tried to dissuade him. The farmer was stubborn. The result was that every one of his lambs exceeded the estimated weight. The next year, in May of 1877, a meeting was held with 19 sheep growers present. William Luton was elected president and Robert A. Cartwright secretary (later president). The new organization vowed to stick together in marketing their lambs, selling only through the club and observing uniform standards of weight and condition. It worked. It was the first

Radnor Lake State Natural Area. The 1000 acres were acquired by the state of Tennessee in 1973. Impounded by a dam built in 1914, the lake covers land over which armies fought in 1864.

such cooperative marketing organization in the United States and it brought new prosperity to Goodlettsville and to stockmen everywhere.

Seventy-five years later there were 850 farmer-owned and farmer-controlled livestock associations in the United States with 939,000 members who sold $1.3 BILLION worth of sheep, hogs, and cattle on an open market. In 1877, in contrast, the market had been tightly controlled by a cabal of buyers who traveled from village to village in the rural South and West acquiring animals on a "take it or leave it" basis.

The Great Country Houses

Two Rivers, in modified Italian Renaissance style, was completed about 1859. David H. McGavock was married to Willie Harding, whose family had built Belle Meade in 1853. The name was given his daughter's mansion by William Harding because of its location near the juncture of Stone's and Cumberland rivers. It is the last great country estate house erected in Davidson County before the Civil War. The owner is now the metropolitan government which uses the house as a conference center.

Three other houses in the county outside Nashville are noteworthy and have played a role in its history. They are Traveller's Rest, Tulip Grove, and Belle Meade.

In or about 1799 Judge John Overton, who was to be Andrew Jackson's political counselor, built a log house on the road leading south from Nashville. Overton in his long career as a lawyer was revenue collector of the Mero District and a member of the state Supreme Court. The house, added to many times, is now a two-storey frame in modified Federal style with the characteristic small front entrance porch leading to a central hall flanked by large receiving rooms. The shuttered windows are also characteristic, as are the chimneys at each end. Many conferences of significance in Tennessee and national politics took place in the house. Later Overton, Jackson, and General James Winchester planned the development of West Tennessee and founded the city of Memphis and Overton moved to West Tennessee.

Tulip Grove, on Lebanon Road across from The Hermitage grounds, was built in 1836 for Andrew Jackson Donelson, secretary and namesake of the president. The designer was Joseph Reiff, who also built The Hermitage in 1835, after a fire damaged the second mansion. Tulip Grove is a brick, two-storey mansion, more comfortable than imposing, but Donelson's career which included service as minister to Prussia and candidate for vice president in 1856, would make his house worthy of notice regardless.

Belle Meade estate was established in 1806 by John Harding. The present house was built in 1853 and its greatest days followed the Civil War. One of the state's great plantations, Belle Meade was one of the earliest Thoroughbred horse breeding farms in America, established by William Giles Harding. It was his son-in-law, General William H. Jackson, whose efforts gave it international fame and brought many distinguished visitors to

Davidson County as well as sending many distinguished horses to race brilliantly and successfully. By 1910 its heyday was over but it has been maintained as a show place by efforts of the Association for Preservation of Tennessee Antiquities since 1954.

Cheekwood is built on a hill. In concept it is eighteenth century England, a stately home. There is a wrought iron stair railing in the oval stairhall that was in Queen Charlotte's Palace at Kew. The Countess of Scarborough once owned the crystal chandeliers. The mahogany doors are from Grosvenor House. But the house is not a copy. It is an original, planned by Bryant Fleming of Ithaca, New York, and begun by Mr. and Mrs. Leslie Cheek in 1929. The house was completed in 1932. The Cheek-Neal Coffee Co. had become successful through Maxwell House Coffee—named for the famous hotel and given the slogan "Good to the last drop!" by President Theodore Roosevelt during his visit to Nashville. The house was inherited by Mrs. Walter Sharp. In 1959 Cheekwood was presented to the state. It was opened to the public in 1960 and is the site of the Tennessee Botanical Gardens and Fine Arts Center.

Distinguished Visitors and Others

More than half of the presidents of the United States have visited Davidson County, or have resided there. In the twentieth century these visitors have included Theodore Roosevelt, William Howard Taft, Woodrow Wilson, Franklin D. Roosevelt, John F. Kennedy, Lyndon B. Johnson, Richard M. Nixon, Gerald Ford, Jimmy Carter, and Ronald Reagan.

Another distinguished twentieth century visitor was the secretary-general of the United Nations, Kurt Waldheim, now president of Austria, who came in 1976 for the first meeting of the United Nations outside New York. Waldheim and his daughter visited Opryland as guests of Governor Ray Blanton, and tried the log flume ride. The year before Opryland had been host to American astronauts and Russian cosmonauts who had just joined in a history-making joint space flight. At Opryland they rode the Wabash Cannonball together.

Wilson was not president of the United States when he came to Nashville on November 29, 1905. As president of Princeton University he was invited to speak to the teachers of the city at Watkins Hall. Although his brother Joseph was an editor of the *Nashville Banner* and his son-in-law William Gibbs McAdoo, later secretary of the treasury, was a native of Tennessee, Wilson did not return to Nashville during his administration. After Taft, the next incumbent president to visit Nashville was Franklin D. Roosevelt in 1934. It was almost thirty years more before another incumbent chief executive would come. John F. Kennedy on May 20, 1963, spoke at Vanderbilt University, lunched with Governor and Mrs. Frank Clement at the governor's mansion on Curtiswood Lane, and visited George Peabody College to inspect the human development laboratory and discuss the visiting professorships supported by the Kennedy Foundation. Lyndon B. Johnson was in Davidson County twice in less than a year. On March 15, 1967, he and Mrs. Johnson came to The Hermitage for the bicentennial of Andrew Jackson's birth, and on June 28, 1968, he returned to dedicate the Percy Priest Dam and Reservoir on Stone's River. Richard Nixon helped dedicate the new Grand Ole Opry House on national television March 16, 1974, played the piano, and was instructed in the art of the yo-yo by Roy Acuff, grand old man of the Opry. His successors, Gerald Ford (1974-77) and Jimmy Carter (1977-81), participated in a joint discussion of American foreign policy at Vanderbilt in 1985; Carter and Ronald Reagan had made campaign stops in 1980.

Indeed it was later learned that a more sinister visitor had stalked Carter during his visit. John Hinckley had been warned by security guards at the airport when he was detected with a weapon. He made a telephone call to an unidentified local number and passed on, to shoot President Reagan in Washington, D.C., soon after Inauguration Day, 1981.

Albert Osborne, who rode a bus to Mexico beside Lee Harvey Oswald in 1963, later resided at the Nashville YMCA, and FBI agents came there to question him when his identity became known to them. Before he could be questioned again, Osborne had gone home to England and died there.

The mother of Sirhan Sirhan, Robert Kennedy's assassin, came to Nashville in 1968 seeking help and mercy for her son. James Earl Ray, Dr. Martin Luther King's assassin, pleaded guilty to the act at the federal courthouse in Nashville and was sentenced to life; part of his term has been served at the state prison.

And there were the James boys. There are fourteen confirmed authentic Frank and Jesse James sites in Davidson County. Some of them are: the house at 606 Boscobel Street where Jesse and Zee James were living in 1875 and where their son Jesse was born; the Walton farm off Clarksville Highway where Frank and Annie James were living in 1877; the Felix Smith place on West Hamilton Avenue where Frank and Jesse and their families lived in 1879; a house at 3111 Hyde's Ferry Pike where Frank and Jesse lived in 1880; Jesse's 1881 residence at 903 Woodland and Frank's at 814 Fatherland; and Jesse's last Tennessee home at 711 Fatherland (most sites have been re-numbered since). Ted Yeatman, authority on the James Brothers, says it is appropriate that the Tennessee Performing Arts Center now stands on the site of Mrs. Kent's boarding house where Jesse lived as John Davis Howard from September to December 1880 because Jesse was always playing a role.

And a man claiming to be Jesse Woodson James himself told his grandchildren in the 1930s (this man lived from 1844 to 1951!) that Nashville had been the Confederate underground capital for nineteen years after Appomattox.

Metroland—John Seigenthaler's Town

He was born and educated in Nashville. In 1949 he began work as a reporter for Silliman Evans' *Nashville Tennessean* and like all young reporters he worked hard to learn the territory. He has held almost every news and editorial position on the newspaper: beat reporter; general assignment reporter covering crime, the courts, local government, the General Assembly, and national politics; feature magazine writer; copy editor; city editor; editor; and publisher. He was a Nieman Fellow at Harvard, a Communications Fellow at Duke, an associate professor of public policy at Duke during the 1980 academic year, and has written two books, *A Search for Justice* and *An Honorable Profession*, both in collaboration with other distinguished journalists.

In 1961 Seigenthaler entered government service, joining the Kennedy administration as administrative assistant to the attorney-general, Robert Kennedy. Working with the U. S. Department of Justice in the fields of organized crime and civil rights, he was the administration's chief negotiator with the governor of Alabama during the 1961 Freedom Rides. During that crisis he was attacked by a mob of white persons and hospitalized with a concussion.

Returning from Washington to become editor of the *Tennessean*, Seigenthaler brought new life to the media, not only in Nashville, not only in Tennessee, but in the South. For the first time a Nashville newspaper could honestly claim parity with the Louisville *Courier-Journal* and the *Memphis Commercial Appeal*. The influence of his office at 1100 Broadway was felt in every part of the state. For the next twenty years Nashville would be John Seigenthaler's town.

The history of Davidson County and Nashville ends in 1962; now it is the story of Metroland. Some of the changes would have come anyway: the lakes, for example, reservoirs created by the large Corps of Engineers dams, Old Hickory and Percy Priest. Not only were thousands of acres put under water, but the shores became the site of new attractive residential developments and recreational areas. A second development was the construction of interstate highways. Nashville was the hub of three of these: 24, 40, and 65, with connecting loops. The proposed outer loop, I-440, was to cause much controversy lasting nearly 20 years as environmentalists chose this for a battleground. A third development was the "Nashville skyline," the sudden development of downtown Nashville into towering office complexes, beginning in 1957 with the Life & Casualty Tower on the corner of Fourth Avenue North and Church Street. And there was the growth and promotion of the music industry, centered in "Music Row," along

Percy Preist Dam on Stone's River was named for the former journalist and Congressman from the "Hermitage District" for a quarter of a century. The reservoir formed by the dam is a popular recreation area. Another is Old Hickory Dam and Reservoir on the Cumberland River.

16th, 17th, and 18th avenues South, near George Peabody College.

Music City replaced Athens of the South as Nashville's promotional pseudonym. The industry was fond of calling the city "the third coast," referring to the established entertainment centers of New York City and Los Angeles. In the 1950s the "Nashville sound" came to be recognized as new and different: Owen Bradley at Bradley's Barn, a recording studio in a rural neighborhood, first introduced echo chambers, drums, and improvised performance. Chet Atkins, already recognized as a talented performer, was a producer for RCA Victor and brought the "sound" to a major label; he also brought famous artists to Nashville to record. Patsy Cline was one of the first to make "crossover" hits: high on both popular and country charts.

Tragedy struck the music community in 1963 and again in 1964 when airplane crashes took her life and those of Hawkshaw

John Hartford is one of
the singers and composers
who began their rise to
fame in Music City, U.S.A.
His first hit was "Gentle
on my Mind."

Hawkins, Cowboy Copas, and musician-executive Randy
Hughes near Camden on March 5, 1963, and Jim Reeves near
Nashville on July 31, 1964. One product of Music City, a native,
succeeded on the pop and gospel side rather than country and
western. Pat Boone got his first pay for singing by leading songs
at a Church of Christ meeting at nearby Gladeville; at 16 he
hosted "Youth on Parade" for WSIX. At 19 he married Shirley
Foley, daughter of country star Red Foley. After winning on "Ar-
thur Godfrey's Talent Scouts," the David Lipscomb graduate rose
to fame like a rocket.

An entertainment landmark is the Belle Meade Theatre on
West End Avenue. Opening in May of 1940, when Edgar Bergen
and Charlie McCarthy played in *Charlie McCarthy, Detective*, the
elegant movie palace features in its front lobby a "Wall of Fame":
photographs signed by stars who have made personal appearances. This was an idea of the first manager, E. J. Jordan.

Another landmark is Mills Book Store, now in three locations, a family store lately owned and operated by Adele Mills Schweid and her husband, Bernie Schweid. An advertisement for the store denied the rumor that Mrs. Schweid was first cradled in a Random House box in the back of Mills, then located on Church Street, but this family business is more than ninety years old and has searched as far as Europe for out-of-print books faithful customers sought. (In 1987 Ron Watkins became proprietor.)

Closely related to the development of the Music City image was the growth of the tourist industry, culminating in the establishment of Opryland U.S.A. on the banks of the Cumberland River eight miles east of the city. Planning began in 1968; in 1972 the amusement park was opened to the public. The new Opry House was opened in March of 1974, with a memorable performance on the yo-yo by President Richard M. Nixon. Opryland Hotel was opened in 1977. In 1983 Gaylord Broadcasting Company of Oklahoma acquired Opryland U.S.A. from American General Insurance Company of Houston, which had taken over National Life.

Not all music personalities have been connected with WSM. John Richbourg was known as "John R." when he ran the first rhythm and blues show on WLAC. He and other "deejays" such as Bill "Hoss" Allen and Gene Noble between 1946 and 1973 had what was believed to have been the largest audience of any record program.

Not all Metro personalities are music-connected. Sheriff Fate Thomas is an example. Each year the sheriff is host to the annual rabbit dinner of the Sure Shot Rabbit Hunters Association, of which the sheriff is president. The first of these events was held in 1954 when twelve hunters got together to eat the product of their hunt. The 32nd was held at the State Fairgrounds and was attended by 5000. Celebrities also, in the world of politics, were the Doyles. Jacobs H. "Jake" Doyle died in 1986. He was the last of the old generation of politicians. Jake Doyle had been chairman of the Civil Service Commission, a Democratic primary election commissioner, and a member of the county Democratic primary board. His sister Frances had been a council member (city and Metro) and a state representative; his brother Andrew J. was a judge of the General Sessions Court; his brother William P. "Pat" Doyle was a councilman and state representative; and his brother Clarence an attorney and forceful advocate. Another celebrity is Police Chief Joe Casey who became president of the International Association of Police Chiefs in 1987.

The adoption of Metro government ended the old style of politics, controlled by ward and district political leaders. Brett Hawkins, historian of the movement for consolidation, says, "The problem in Nashville was Ben West and annexation, and the solution was Metro." He sets up various candidates for the real power behind the movement for consolidation: the Citizens' Committee for Better Government, James H. Roberson, the *Tennessean*, "professional politicians" who took over the movement after the failed effort of 1958, and eliminates each in turn as the key power. It was West, he decides, and the "green sticker," that was the catalyst. The sticker was applied to an automobile windshield to indicate payment of a wheel or "use" tax for which county as well as city residents were liable. In 1961 the General Assembly passed an act authorizing a referendum to create a new Charter Commission; the proposal passed August 17, 1961. The charter commission that was then established included Cecil Branstetter, R. N. Chenault, Carmack Cochran, K. Harlan Dodson, Jr., Victor S. Johnson, Z. Alexander Looby, G. S. Meadors, Rebecca Thomas, Joe E. Torrence, and Charles Warfield. Edwin F. Hunt was legal counsel.

George H. Cate, Jr., chairman of the Citizens' Committee for Better Government, was not a member but in the campaign that preceded the referendum of June 28, 1962, was an especially effective speaker. The vote in favor of Metro was 36,978 to 28,103. After the suit of *Frazier* vs. *Carr* was settled by opinions of Chancellor Glenn W. Woodlee and the state Supreme Court upholding the constitutionality of consolidation, the voters on November 6 and 27 elected Beverly Briley mayor, George Cate vice-mayor, and a council of forty persons.

After the civil rights campaign gained desegregation of public schools and public facilities, many in the white community

NOTICE
ALL PERSONS AND
PARCELS SUBJECT TO
THOROUGH INSPECTION

In 1960 WSM-TV showed live the hostage crisis at the Tennessee State Prison. Announcer Jud Collins holds the microphone. (photo from TV screen)

believed the progress made was sufficient. During the middle 1960s however court-ordered busing to achieve racial balance in the public schools stirred controversy once more. Black voters had never been denied access to the polls, although the state poll tax did hinder voter participation by the poor, black and white. Busing affected the white suburban middle class most of all. Black organizations focused on Davidson County. NAACP, SCLC, CORE, SNCC, Black Muslim, all, from moderate to radical, were represented. Street demonstrations were their weapon. In the spring of 1964, again in April of 1967, after a controversial visit by militant activist Stokely Carmichael, and once more in April of 1968, after the assassination of Dr. Martin Luther King, violence gripped the city. As time passed the tension relaxed. The 1970s sought solutions rather than the confrontations that Saul Alinsky, community organizer who spoke at the Peabody summer lectures in 1967, had advocated. Alinsky had said that social progress comes only through divisiveness. But it would be environmentalism and rock music that would stir emotions, not civil rights. By 1974 conditions had so much changed that the Race Relations Information Center closed.

Influential leaders of the black community have included Dr. Z. Alexander Looby and Senator Avon T. Williams, attorneys; the Rev. Kelly Miller Smith, Sr., pastor of the First Baptist Church, Capitol Hill; Robert Lillard, the first black trial judge in Nashville; Coyness Ennix, member of the county board of education; J. C. Napier, nineteenth century financier, city councilman, and registrar of the U. S. Treasury; Dr. Dorothy Brown, surgeon; Eva Lowery Bowman, businesswoman and organizer of the Southwest Civic League.

Davidson County sent two ambassadors to Europe: in 1969, Guilford Dudley, former chairman of Life & Casualty Insurance Company, was appointed ambassador to Denmark. Joe M. Rodgers, finance chairman of President Reagan's Committee to Re-Elect the President and a successful general contractor, was appointed ambassador to France in 1985.

Although Rodgers and Dudley are among Metro's wealthiest, it is Ray Danner who is listed by *Forbes Magazine* as one of the wealthiest in America. The chairman of Shoney's opened his first restaurant in Madison Square shopping center in 1959; now he is worth an estimated $175 million. Jack Massey of Nashville was on the list in 1984, with a fortune estimated at $150 million. He has made many large gifts to Belmont College.

The Department of Commerce estimates that by the year 2000 Metro's population will exceed one million and the per capita income will be $15,454, an increase of 39.8 percent over 1983, the third highest increase in the nation.

By 1983 the largest private employer, according to the Nashville Area Chamber of Commerce, was Vanderbilt with 6630 persons, slightly more than Hospital Corporation of America, 6500. South Central Bell employed 4500; AVCO, 4215; Opryland, 4175; and Kroger, 2960. Government employees were by far the largest bloc however: state, federal, Metro, and Metro schools

One of Davidson County's most distinguished lawyers of the twentieth century was Z. Alexander Looby. He is shown seated at defense counsel's table *(second from left)* in a 1954 murder trial. (photo by Neal Blackburn)

together employed over 42,000 persons! Besides AVCO, only four purely industrial employers in Metroland hired more than 1000 workers. They were DuPont, Genesco, Ford Glass, and Aladdin.

In September of 1985 the grand opening of One Nashville Place was held. The 23-storey glass and granite office tower might have been one of the "towers of Zenith" described by novelist Sinclair Lewis. A dozen exhibits of Metro's progress were displayed in the lobby: one for Riverfront Park, another for the Summer Lights festival; a model of the new airport. There was none for Lower Broad.

Tootsie's Orchid Lounge is a symbol of what Lower Broad used to be while the Ryman housed the Opry. It was a fabled barroom for country musicians who could come out of the back door of the Ryman and into the back door of Tootsie's where Hattie Louise Bess presided until her death in 1978. After the Opry moved away from the Ryman, the area decayed, although some stubborn businesses have clung to their locations between Fifth and First. Symptomatic of one problem, according to an article in *The Nashville Banner*, was The Fish Net, a haven for transients and street people which closed in June of 1986. A Music Row lawyer who gave free legal aid to some of the transients pointed to alcohol and drugs and their easy availability as the central problem. "Where there are poor people there are problems that cause their poverty," said the Rev. Bill Barnes, pastor who spends much of his time ministering to the needs of the underclass. Besides the Edgehill United Methodist Church, where he is assigned, efforts to combat poverty are forwarded by the Christian Cooperative Ministry, the East Nashville Cooperative Ministry, the Holy Name Church, the Woodmont Baptist Church, Belmont United Methodist Church, and the Salvation Army.

In considering other problems the International Leadership Center of Dallas conducted a survey of Metro that saw planning as the vital need. It found the 1980 General Plan, intended to serve twenty years ahead, already obsolete. The decision by American Airlines to make Nashville a regional hub was seen as having the most profound impact on growth. The survey found that decisions irrevocably affecting the whole community have been made within a tight-knit business community while the music industry, the universities, the several ethnic communities, and the blue-collar commmunity have been largely excluded. One major problem is the decay of the water and sewer system that underlies downtown: the cost of replacing it has been estimated at $700 million. Said the *Tennessean*: "There is more to development and renovation than just putting up pretty new buildings and sitting back and collecting the rent from them." But in one of his last interviews Mayor Briley took a more balanced view of Metro:

Tootsie's Orchid Lounge on Lower Broadway near the Ryman was a celebrated gathering place for Opry artists and fans.

"It has an usual culture. It has a great warmth among its people. It has a tradition of respect for law and order, heavier than most cities. It has a good economic base of being so diverse, never any one or two or three industries can claim ownership of it. It has a broad-based power structure that comes from a completely unusual economic society; then the fact that we have so many universities here gives it a more educated middle class. I don't mean there are not extremes where there is not that good an education—but as a whole the middle class here is better educated than you'll find in a lot of places and that's especially true of the black part of the community. That's very healthful. In addition the broad base of the religious organizations that have their headquarters here have brought people into the community who are good social thinkers. That's rather unusual for a city."

Sports is often seen as a metaphor for American life. Here were three success stories: Roy Skinner, following Bob Polk, made Vanderbilt a major basketball power; Larry Schmittou brought professional baseball back with a genius for attracting large crowds to Greer Stadium to watch the Sounds; and Steve Sloan electrified Commodore football fans by making Vanderbilt a real contender in the Southeastern Conference. The old Nashville Vols who had played in Sulphur Dell since 1885 closed out that era in 1963, winning their last game in the Southern Association but before a mere handful of loyal fans. Brighter was the picture in the 1984 Olympic Games, when swimmer Tracy Caulkins brought three gold medals home to Metro. And the first quarter-century of Metro ended on a high note: the David Lipscomb College basketball team won the national championship in the 1986 NAIA tournament at Kansas City.

In 1972 John Seigenthaler became publisher and in 1978 president of Tennessean Newspapers, Inc. In 1982, after the Gannett company bought the *Tennessean* he was given the additional assignment of editorial director of *USA Today*. His interest in the profession of letters led to a television program, "A Word on Words," for the Southern Public Television Network. He was a participant and a moderator of the Cumberland Writers Conference, and in 1986 received an honorary Doctor of Humane Letters degree from Cumberland University. His other personal awards include the Sidney Hillman Prize for Courage in Publishing, the National Headliner Award for Investigative Reporting, and the Pi Delta Epsilon national Medal of Merit. He was awarded the 1981 Mass Media Award of the American Jewish committee, was elected a Sigma Delta Chi Fellow, and the First Amendment Chair of Excellence has been established at Middle Tennessee State University in his name. Not only is Metroland Mr. Seigenthaler's town: his influence is felt far beyond its borders.

Governors From Davidson County

Remarkably, there have been few governors of Tennessee who could be claimed as natives or residents of Davidson County at the time of their election. Not until William Carroll, the fifth governor (1821–1827, 1829–1835), was a resident of Davidson County an occupant of the governor's chair. He was a native of

Pennsylvania and came to Nashville as a young man, becoming a hardware merchant. He was also one of Andrew Jackson's officers in the Creek War. His old comrades in arms, like Jackson's, stood by him and formed a dependable political nucleus.

In 1827 Governor Carroll was constitutionally unable to seek reelection. Another resident of Davidson County succeeded him: Samuel Houston, born in Virginia, reared in Blount County, briefly at home with the Cherokees, then a soldier with Jackson in the Creek War, in which he was wounded. Becoming a lawyer he practiced at Lebanon until elected district attorney, when he moved to Nashville. He was elected to Congress from what later came to be called the Hermitage District in 1823 and 1825. He was elected governor in 1827 and it was conceded that, as a protege of General Jackson, there was no limit to his political future: "First Jackson will be president, then Houston." The shocking end of the marriage between Governor Houston and young Eliza Allen, still not satisfactorily explained, finished, it was thought, Houston's career. But he did become president—of the Republic of Texas, whose independence General Houston assured at the Battle of San Jacinto on March 17, 1836.

Jackson, of course, although he had been military governor of Florida, was never governor of Tennessee. The next resident of Davidson County to serve as chief executive was Neill S. Brown. (It is sometimes said that James Chamberlain Jones was born in Davidson County. He was born at Fountain of Health, a resort on the Wilson-Davidson county line; although the post office for the resort hamlet was in Davidson County, Jones' birthplace was east of the line.) Governor Brown was born in Giles County, but spent his adult life in Nashville. He served as a soldier in the Seminole War and held elective office as a legislator, a presidential elector (he was a Whig), governor (1847–1849), speaker of the state House of Representatives, and member of the 1870 state constitutional convention. He also was minister to Russia.

William Bowen Campbell reversed Neill Brown's experience in that he was born in Davidson County, but spent most of his adult life elsewhere, chiefly in Smith and Wilson counties (his residence in Lebanon is listed on the National Register of Historic Places). He was governor in 1851–1853.

James D. Porter was born at Paris in Henry County and Paris may properly claim him as a resident because of his long practice of law there, but after his service as governor (1875–1881) he became president of the Nashville, Chattanooga & St. Louis Railroad, then served President Grover Cleveland as assistant secretary of state, after which he became successively a trustee of the Peabody Educational Fund, a trustee of the University of Nashville, and finally chancellor of the Peabody Normal College, successor institution of the University of Nashville. Porter died at Paris in 1912.

Although John P. Buchanan, governor in 1891–1893, was a great-grandson of Major John Buchanan, pioneer and founder of the famous Buchanan's Fort in Davidson County, he was a resident of Rutherford County. And although James B. Frazier, governor in 1903–1905, was a son of Judge Thomas N. Frazier, for many years judge of the criminal court of Davidson County, he was properly a resident of Hamilton County. Albert H. Roberts, governor in 1919–1921, was a native of Overton County and chancellor of the fourth division until he became a candidate for governor in 1918. He remained in Davidson County after his term and his residence at Donelson, high on a hill overlooking that community, was a landmark of eastern Davidson County.

The last resident of Davidson County to serve as governor was Hill McAlister (1933–1937). A lawyer, he had served several terms as state treasurer, experience useful during the times of financial crisis in which he was inaugurated. His terms coincided with the first term of President Franklin D. Roosevelt and the New Deal. He was elected in one of the most bitterly contested primaries held in the state since the split over Prohibition, defeating Lewis Pope only because of a heavy majority in E. H. Crump's Memphis. His administrations marked the beginning of Crump's sixteen-year hegemony. Nevertheless he was not an unsuccessful administrator: he saw that state expenditures were reduced, a committee began an exhaustive study of public education, and a system of state parks was developed. He was born in 1875 and died in 1960.

Frank G. Clement (1953–1959; 1963–1967) became a resident of Davidson County after his service as governor, but he was elected from Dickson County. After his third term as governor ended, he began the practice of law in Nashville but was killed in an automobile accident in 1969.

Hugh Walker *(left)*, newspaperman and official Davidson County historian until his death in 1986, and Dixon Merritt, former editor of the Nashville *Tennessean*, were authors of books on Tennessee history.

Suggested Readings

Adams, George Rollie, and Ralph Jerry Christian. *Nashville: A Pictorial History.* Virginia Beach: Donning, 1980.

Amis, Reese. *History of the 114th Field Artillery.* Nashville: Benson, 1920.

Beard, W. E. *It Happened in Nashville, Tennessee.* Nashville, 1912.

Brandau, Roberta Seawell. *History of the Homes and Gardens of Tennessee.* Nashville: Garden Study Club, 1936; rpt. 1964.

Caldwell, Mary French. *Andrew Jackson's Hermitage.* Nashville, 1933.

Clayton, W. W. *History of Davidson County, Tennessee.* Philadelphia: Lewis, 1880.

Conkin, Paul K. *Gone with the Ivy: A Biography of Vanderbilt University.* Knoxville: University of Tennessee Press, 1985.

Crabb, Alfred Leland. *Nashville: Personality of a City.* Indianapolis: Bobbs Merrill, 1960.

Creighton, Wilbur Foster. *Building of Nashville.* Nashville, 1969.

Crutchfield, James A. *Footprints Across the Pages of Tennessee History.* Nashville: Williams, 1976.

Davis, Louise Littleton. *Nashville Tales.* Gretna, Louisiana: Pelican, 1981.

Douglas, Byrd. *Steamboatin' on the Cumberland.* Nashville: Tennessee Book Co., 1961.

Doyle, Don H. *Nashville in the New South, 1880–1920.* Knoxville: University of Tennessee Press, 1985.

———. *Nashville Since the 1920s.* Knoxville: University of Tennessee Press, 1985.

Durham, Walter T. *Nashville: The Occupied City, 1862–1863.* Nashville: Tennessee Historical Society, 1986.

Edgerton, John, ed. *Nashville: The Faces of Two Centuries, 1780–1980.* Nashville: PlusMedia, 1979.

Gower, Herschel. *Pen and Sword: The Life and Journals of Randal W. McGavock.* early journals, Gower, ed.; (political and Civil War journals, Jack Allen, ed.)

Graham, Eleanor, ed. *Nashville: A Short History and Selected Buildings.* Nashville: Metro Historical Commission, 1974.

Hawkins, Brett W. *Nashville Metro: The Politics of City-County Consolidation.* Nashville: Vanderbilt University Press, 1966.

Hearne, Mary Glenn, coordinator. *Nashville: A Family Town.* Nashville: The Nashville Room, Public Library, 1978.

Hoobler, James A., ed. *Nashville Memories: Thirty-Two Historic Postcards.* Knoxville: University of Tennessee Press, 1983.

Horn, Stanley. *The Decisive Battle of Nashville.* Baton Rouge: Louisiana State University Press, 1956.

Huddleston, Ed. *Big Wheels and Little Wagons.* Nashville: Nashville Banner, 1960.

Norman, Jack. *The Nashville I Knew.* Nashville: Rutledge Hill, 1984.

Putnam, Albigence W. *History of Middle Tennessee, or Life and Times of General James Robertson.* 1859. rpt. Knoxville: University of Tennessee Press, 1971.

Remini, Robert V. *Andrew Jackson and the Course of American Empire: 1767–1821.* New York: Harper & Row, 1981. *Andrew Jackson and the Course of American Freedom: 1822–1832.* New York: Harper & Row, 1981. *Andrew Jackson and the Course of American Democracy: 1833–1845.* New York: Harper & Row, 1984.

Russell, Fred. *Bury Me in an Old Press Box.* New York: Barnes, 1957.

Seven Early Churches of Nashville. Intro. Alfred Leland Crabb. Lectures: H. T. Tipps: J. E. Windrow; Walter Stokes, Jr.; Herman Burns; Joseph Green, Jr.; Loren Williams; Msgr. Charles M. Williams; Wayne H. Bell; Fedora Small Frank. Nashville: Elder's, 1972.

Tennessee: A Guide to the State. Federal Writers Project. New York: Viking, 1939.

Thomas, Jane H. *Old Days in Nashville.* Nashville: Publishing House, Methodist Episcopal Church, South, 1897.

Walker, Hugh. *Tennessee Tales.* Nashville: Aurora, 1970.

Wallace, Louis D., ed. *Makers of Millions.* Nashville: Tennessee Department of Agriculture, 1951.

Waller, William, editor. *Nashville in the 1890s.* Nashville: Vanderbilt University Press, 1970.

_____. *Nashville: 1900 to 1910.* Nashville: Vanderbilt University Press, 1972.

White, Robert H., ed. *Tennessee, Old and New.* Sesquicentennial Edition. 2 vols. Nashville: Tennessee Historical Commission, 1946.

Williams, Samuel Cole. *Tennessee During the Revolutionary War.* Nashville: Tennessee Historical Commission, 1944.

Wolfe, Charles K. *The Grand Ole Opry: The Early Years.* London: Old Time Music, 1975.

Woolridge, John. *History of Nashville, Tennessee, 1890;* rpt. Charles Elder, 1970.

Young, R. A. *Reminiscences.* Nashville: Methodist Publishing House, 1900.

Zibart, Carl. *Yesterday's Nashville.* Miami: Seeman, 1976.

Index

Illustrations are indicated by an asterisk following the page number.

Acklen, Mrs. Joseph A. S., 32
Acuff, Roy, 88, 110
Agar, Herbert, 77
Agriculture, 10, 23, 36–37, 38–39, 47, 105, 106–107
Aiken, Leona Taylor, 80
Alden, Augustus E., 50–51
Allen, Bill "Hoss," 115
Allen, Eliza, 20–22, 123
Allen, Robert, 21
American, The, 64, 65, 69
Amqui Railway Station, 79*
Andrews, Frank W., 89
Antioch, 79, 101, 102–103
Armistice, false, 92–93
Armstrong, Robert, 23
Atkins, Chet, 113
Attack on Leviathan, The, 77
Automobile, impact of, 100

Back, Jacques, 76
Bailey, Deford, 75
Baltz, Robert, 104
Banks, 15, 16, 80–81, 86
Barnes, Bill, 120
Barry, Daniel, 62
Barton, Gabriel, 11
Barton, Samuel, 10–12
Bass, John M., 51
Bell, Albert, 83
Bell, John, 25
Bell, Montgomery, 60
Belle Meade, 79, 107, 108–109
Belle Meade Theatre, 114
Bellevue, 101, 103–104
Belmont, 31–32, 44, 98–99
Belmont College, 32, 98–99
Belmont United Methodist Church, 120
Berry, Harry S., 81
Blackemore, J. J., 11
Blanton, Ray, 109

Blacks, 12, 37, 42, 48–50, 51, 100–101, 116–118
Bledsoe, Isaac, 11
Blount, William, 12, 14
Bluefields, 79–80
Bluffs, battle of the, 7
Boone, Pat, 114
Bontemps, Arna, 49
Bowling, William K., 53–54
Bowman, Eva Lowery, 118
Bradley, Owen, 113
Branstetter, Cecil, 116
Briley, Beverly, 97, 116, 120–121
Brown, Dorothy, 118
Brown, James S., 69
Brown, Neill S., 51, 123
Brown, Paul, 96
Brown, Randall, 51
Buchanan, John, and fort, 9, 124
Bumpass, Ruth, 96
Burr, Aaron, 15

Cain-Sloan, 85–86
Caldwell, Rogers, 80–81
Campbell, William Bowen, 123
Candyland, 85*
Cannon, Mrs. Henry, 88
Capitol building, 27, 28*, 55, 62, 63
Carmack, Edward Ward, 64–66, 69
Carroll, William, 17, 19–20, 23, 122–123
Carter, Jimmy, 110
Cartwright, Robert A., 106
Casey, Joe, 116
Castner-Knott, 85–86
Cate, George H. Jr., 116
Caulkins, Tracy, 122
Centennial Park, 35
Centennials, 62–63
Central Tennessee College, 50
Chambers- Turrentine house, 9
Cheatham, Benjamin Franklin, 51, 57

Cheatham, Leonard P., 23
Cheek, Mr. & Mrs. Leslie, 109
Cheekwood, 109
Chenault, R. N., 116
Christian Cooperative Ministry, 120
Civil War, 39–47, 105, 106; battles, 42–46
Clark, George Rogers, 6
Clarke, Lardner, 12
Clay, Henry, 33
Clement, Frank G., 110, 125
Cliffe, D. B., 35
Cline, Patsy, 113
Clover Bottom, 6, 43, 80, 101, 104
Cochran, Carmack, 116
Cocke, William, 14
Cockrill, Mark Robertson, 35–37, 106
Coffee, John, 104
Cole, Edmund W., 58, 59
Cole, Maggie Porter, 48–49
Colyar, A. S., 51
Commercial, 64
Consolidation, city-county, 97, 112, 116
Cooper, Duncan, 64–66
Cooper, Robin, 65–66
Copas, Cowboy, 114
Couchville, 43, 79
Covered bridge, the, 20, 21*
Craighead, Thomas, 12
Creighton, Wilbur F., 64
Croft, Elise and Margaret, 9
Cumberland College, 15, 18, 19, 59
Cumberland Compact, the, 10–12
Cumberland Park, 68
Cummings, Thomas L., 97
Curry, Walter Clyde, 75

Dandrige, E. W., 46
Danner, Ray, 118
Daugherty, Edward, 72
David Lipscomb College, 122
Davidson, Donald, 73, 75, 77
Davidson, William Lee, 3–4
Davidson Academy, 11–12, 15, 18
Davidson County: communities of, 8–10,
    101–109; creation of, 7–8; geography,
    1–2; map, 2*; population (in 1795) 12,
    (in 1830s) 23, (in 1980) 3, (in 2000)
    118; visitors to, 109–111
Davis, Andrew, 16
Decker, John, 26
Democrat, the, 64, 65
Democrats, 33, 50, 56, 64–65, 66, 67–68.
    See also Politics.

Demonbreun. *See* Montbrun, Jacques
    Timothe Boucher de.
Desegregation, 100–101, 116–118
DeWitt, Jack, 93
Dickerson, Isaac, 49
Dickinson, Charles, 15
Dilzer, Mrs. I. B., 96
Dodson, K. Harlan Jr., 116
Donelson, 80, 101–102, 124
Donelson, Andrew Jackson, 108
Donelson, John, 6–7, 10
Donelson, Rachel, 14
Doyle, Andrew, 116
Doyle, Clarence, 116
Doyle, Frances, 115–116
Doyle, Jacobs H. "Jake," 115
Doyle, William P. "Pat," 116
Drake, Brittain, 20
Driver, William, 41
Dudley, Guilford, 118
Dudley, Richard Houston, 69
Dunn, Michael G., 9
Dupontonia, 70

Eagle Tavern, 22
Early settlers, 6, 8–9, 10, 11, 12
East Nashville Cooperative Ministry, 120
Eaton, John, 17
Edgefield: battle at, 43; junction, 79
Edgehill United Methodist Church, 120
Edgerton, John, 67
Education, 11–12, 15, 18, 38, 47, 48–50,
    56, 59–62, 94, 95*, 97–99, 100–101
El Chico! (musical group), 95–96
Elliott, C. D., 62
Elliott, Mary Organ, 95
Elliott, William Yandall, 75
Elm Crag, 102, 104–105
Employment, 118–119
Ennix, Coyness, 118
Epidemics: cholera, 24, 30, 31, 53–54;
    influenza, 70–71
Eskew, Herman, 86
Estes, Claudine, 95
Evans, Green, 49
Evans, Silliman, 111
Ewin, Andrew, 11
Ewing, Edwin H., 27

Fanning, Tolbert, 104–105
Field, M. D., 31
Fillmore, Millard, 37

First Presbyterian Church, 28–30, 29*
Fish Net, The, 120
Fisk University, 48–50, 100
Fletcher, John Gould, 77
Fogg, Francis B., 23
Foley, Shirley, 114
Ford, Gerald, 110
Ford, Whitey, 88
Forrest, Nathan Bedford, 42
Fort, Cornelia, 89
Frank, James M., house, 76*
Franklin College, 104–105
Franklin, Adelicia Hayes, 31–32
Franklin, state of, 8
Frazier, Thomas N., 124
Freeland, George, 11
Freemasonry, 17–18
French, 4–5
French Lick, 5, 6, 7
Frierson, William, 76
Fry, S. S., 35
Fugitive, The, 75, 76–77
Fugitives, the, 75–77
Fugitives: An Anthology, 77

George Peabody College for Teachers, 50, 62, 100, 110
Gibbs, George W., 17–18
Gladeville, 114
Gleaves family, 10
"Good Government" movement, 67, 68–69
Goodlettsville, 79, 102, 105–107
Goodlettsville Lamb and Wool Club, 106–107
Gordon, Louisa Pocahontas, 32
Gower, Herschel, 95
Gower, Jennie Lou, 89, 95–96
Grace Presbyterian Church, 66*
Grand Ole Opry, 72, 74–75, 88, 92, 110
Granny White Market, 102*
Grassmere House, 9
Green, A. L. P., 59
Grundy, Felix, 23, 25, 31
Guild, George, 68
Guild, Joseph Conn, 51

Hall, Allen A., 26, 37
Harding, William Giles, 108
Harding, Willie, 107
Harkreader, Sidney Johnson, 74, 75
Harpeth Hall School, 99

Harris, Isham G., 64
Harris, Mrs. Weaver, 95
Hart, Freeland, and Roberts, 78
Hartford, John, 114*
Harvey, Fred, 84–86
Hatch, Stephen D., 49
Hatton, Mrs. Robert, 47
Hawkins, Brett, 116
Hawkins, Hawkshaw, 113–114
Hay, George D., 74
Haywood, John, 16
Head, James M., 69
Healey, George H. P., 30
Heaton, Amos, 8
Heiman, Adolphus, 27, 31
Henderson, Richard, 6, 7, 10–11
Hermitage, The, 43, 104, 108, 110
Heron, Susan, 98–99
Hickman, Litton, 96–97
Hinckley, John, 110
Hirsch, Sidney Mttron, 75, 76
Hoggatt, John, 104
Hoggatt family, 80
Holmes, Benjamin M., 49
Holy Name Church, 120
Hood, Ida, 98–99
Hooper, Clifford E., 104
Horn, Stanley, 70
Hospitals, 89
Houston, Sam, 16, 17–18, 20–22, 24, 30, 123
Howard School, 38
Howell, Morton, 96
Howell, Morton B., 55
Howse, Hilary, 67–69, 81, 97
Hughes, Randy, 114
Hunt, Edwin F., 116
Hunt, William G., 26
Hutchings, John, 104

Ice storm, great, 96
I'll Take My Stand, 77
Indians, 4–5, 7, 25
Industry, 23, 38, 70, 89, 119, 120; early mills, 8–9, 10, 38
Irish, 69
Iroquois Steeplechase, 86

Jackson, Andrew, 6, 13–16, 17, 19, 21, 24, 30, 104, 108, 110, 123; houses of, 15*, 26*; equestrian statue of, 62–63
Jackson, Jennie, 49

Jackson, William H., 108
Jarrell, Randall, 78
James, Frank and Jesse, 111
Johns, Charles D., 69
Johnson, Andrew, 39, 42, 46, 51–53, 54
Johnson, Lyndon B., 110
Johnson, Stanley, 75
Johnson, Victor S., 116
Jones, James Chamberlain, 33, 123
Jones, (Thomas?), 6
Jordan, E. J., 114
Jubilee Hall, 49
Jubilee Singers, 48–49

Kasper, John, 101
Kelley, A. Z., 100–101
Kelley, David Campbell, 47, 59
Kennedy, John F., 110
Kenyon Review, 77
Kercheval, Thomas A., 55–56, 68
Killebrew, Mrs. James, 95
Kinney, Belle, 72, 79
Kirkland, James H., 61
Kline, Henry Blue, 77
Ku Klux Klan, 48

Lafayette, Marquis de, 16
Lanier, Lyle, 77
Lapsley, R. A., 62
Lawrence, Nathanael, 19
Lea, Luke, 71, 73, 80–81
Lebeck Bros., 84–85, 86
Legislative Plaza, 72
Lewis, E. C., 63
Lillard, Robert, 118
Lind, Jenny, 37
Lindsley, Isaac, 11
Lindsley, J. Berrien, 51, 59
Lindsley, Nathanael Lawrence, 19
Lindsley, Philip, 18–19, 59
Lindsley Avenue Church of Christ, 66*
Litterer, William, 68
Looby, Z. Alexander, 116, 118, 119*
Loss, Alice, 93
Louisville & Nashville RR, 58–59
Luton, William, 106
Lytle, Andrew, 76, 77

McAllister, Hill, 124–125
McCarthy, William, 68
McCarver, Charles P. 68
McGavock, David, 107

McGavock, Frank and Hugh, 38
McGavock, Randal, 37
McGavock, Randal William, 37, 38
McGavock properties, 80
McGugin, Dan, 66–67
McKee, John Miller, 40, 41
McKinley, William, 63
McMurray family, 80
McNairy, John, 14
McTyeire, Holland, 59
McWhortersville, 102, 105
Macon, Uncle Dave, 74
Mallory, Thomas, 11
Marling, John Leake, 34
Masonic Lodge, first, 15
Massey, Jack, 118
Mauldin, James, 11
Maynard, Horace, 51
Maxon, Helen and Howard, 102
Maxwell House, the, 48, 51, 53, 109
Meadors, G. S., 116
Medical School of University of
    Nashville, 61–62
Meharry, Hugh, Samuel and
    Alexander, 50
Meharry Medical College, 50
Mental hospital, 20, 24
Merritt, Dixon, 125*
Merritt, Lanier, 95
Merritt, John, 101
Meteor shower, 25
Mill Springs, battle of, 35, 39
Mills Book Store, 114–115
Mills, Clark, 62
Mims, Edwin, 75
Minnie Pearl. *See* Cannon, Mrs. Henry.
Monroe, James, 16
Montbrun, Jacques Timothe
    Boucher de, 5–6
Montgomery Bell Academy, 60, 61, 94
Moore, John Trotwood, 76
Moore, Merrill, 79
Morgan, John Hunt, 42
Morgan, Sam, 33
Morgan, Samuel Dodd, 54–55
Morris, K. J., 51
Morris, Thomas O., 69
Mott, Hugh, 92
Music City, 113–115.
    See also "Opry Town."

Naff, Mrs. L. C., 88
Napier, J. C., 118

Nash, Francis, 3
Nashborough, Fort, 1, 3, 11
Nashville, 13, (in 1788) 14, (1824) 37, (in
    1830s) 23, (in 1850s) 37–39, (in 1920s)
    72–73, (in 1930s) 83–84; bankruptcy,
    50–51; downtown, 99–100, 112–113,
    119–120; fall of, 40–41; fires, 37, 70,
    82; government, 37–38, 51, 68–69, 97;
    Music Row, 112–113; population, 37;
    reservoir, 69–70
Nashville & Chattanooga RR, 37, 58
Nashville Bridge Co., 89
Nashville Female Academy, 19, 62, 98
Nashville Gas-Light Co., 57
Nashville Symphony, 72
Nashville Vols, 122
Nashville, battle of, 44–46, 57;
    monument, 45*
Nashville, Chattanooga & St. Louis RR,
    58, 70, 79, 124
Natchez Trace Restaurant, 103, 104
New Deal, 81, 124
New Orleans, battle of, 16
Newspapers, 26, 64, 65, 83, 103, 110,
    111–112, 120, 122
Nichol, Josiah, 24
Nicholson, A. O. P., 32
Nixon, H. C., 77
Nixon, Richard, 110, 115
Noble, Gene, 115
Noel, Eleanor Crawford, 95
Nolen, William, 9
Nolensville, 9
Norman, Jack, reminiscences of, 83–84
Norvell, C. C., 26
Nye, S., 26

Old Central, 60*
"Old Glory," 41
Old Hickory Dam, 112
Old Hickory powder plant, 70
Olympic winners, 101, 122
"Opry Town," 73–84. See also Music City.
Opryland U.S.A., 109, 110, 115, 118
Ore Expedition, 12–13
Osborne, Albert, 110-111
Otey, James, 35
Overton, John, 108
Overton family, 10
Owsley, Frank, 77

Parthenon, 64*, 78, 78*

Patterson, Josiah, 65
Patterson, Malcolm "Ham," 65, 66, 68
Payne, Bruce Ryburn, 62
Payne, John Howard, 32
Payne, William H., 61
Peabody Normal College, 61, 124
Percy Priest Dam and Reservoir,
    110, 112, 113*
Percy Warner Park, 81, 86
Petway Reavis Bldg., 52*
Peyton, Balie Jr., 35
Phillips, C. Hooper, 55–56
Plimpton, Clara C., 57–58
Poindexter, George, 37
Politics, 25, 32–33, 34, 50, 51–53, 56,
    64–66, 67–69, 96–97, 116
Polk, James K., 30–31, 33, 53
Polk, Sarah Childress, 31
Porter, James D., 61, 124
Postage stamps, 30
Potter, Edward Jr., 86
Price, Andrew, 104
Prison, state, 20, 23–24
Progressives, 50
Prohibition, 65, 69
Prostitution, 46

Radio, impact of, 73
Radnor Lake State Natural Area, 107*
Railroad bridge, 38, 41
Railroads, 37, 38, 58–59, 70
Ransom, John Crowe, 75, 77
Ray, James Earl, 111
Reconstruction, 47–48, 50–53, 56
Recreational areas, 107, 112, 113
Redevelopment projects, 93–94
Reeves, Jim, 114
Reform period, 67–73
Reiff, Joseph, 108
Remagan Bridge, 92
Republican party, 55
Richbourg, John, 115
Riding, Laura, 76
Roads, 9, 10, 16, 20, 23, 112
Roberts, Albert H., 124
Robertson, Charlotte Reeves, 7
Robertson, James, 5, 6, 7, 11, 12, 14, 57
Robertson Association, 38
Rodgers, Joe M., 118
Roger Williams University, 50, 61
Roosevelt, Franklin D., 81, 110, 124
Roosevelt, Theodore, 109
Rounsevall, David, 11

Rubin, Louis, 77
Rudolph, Wilma, 101
Rutling, Thomas, 49
Ryman, Thomas G., 87
Ryman Auditorium, 72, 74, 87*–88, 120

Sacred Harp, The, 13
Salvation Army, 120
Sangster's Tavern, 10
Schmittou, Larry, 121-122
Scholz, Leopold, 72, 79
Schools, *See* Education.
Schweid, Bernie and Adele Mills, 115
Scott, W. A., 62
Scovel, H. G., 51
Second Army Maneuvers, 90–92, 91*
Seigenthaler, John, 111–112, 122
Shaw, James, 11
Sheep raising, 35–37, 106–107
Shelby, John, 38
Sheppard, Ella, 49
Shy's Hill, 44
"Sit-ins," 100
Skinner, Roy, 121
Sloan, Steve, 122
Smith, Charles G., 51
Smith, E. Kirby, 60
Smith, Kelly Miller Sr., 118
Smith, Reese Jr., 102
Souby, Susan, 99
Southern Convention, 37
"Southern Courthouse Town, A," 54–67
Sports, 66–67, 83, 101, 121–122
Stanford, A. F. and R. D., 79–80, 104
Starr, Alfred, 76
State Normal College, 60, 61
Steamboats, 19–20
Stearns, Eben S., 60
Stevenson, Alec Brock, 75
Stevenson, Vernon K., 58
Stoner, Michael, 6
Strickland, William, 27–28
Stump, Frederick, 8–9
Suburban development, 79–80,
    103–104, 112
Suspension bridge, first, 31, 41

TV, 117*, 122
TVA, 81
Tannehill, Wilkins, 17–18
Tarbox School, 56*
Tate, Allen, 76, 77
Tate, Minnie, 49

Taylor, Donald, 93
Taylor, Robert L., 63, 65
Temple, Ed, 101
Tennessee A & I College, 94
Tennessee Centennial Exposition, 63, 78
Tennessee State University, 100, 101
Thomas, Fate, 115
Thomas, John W., 63
Thomas, Rebecca, 116
Thompson, Hugh, 87
Thompson, "Uncle Jimmy," 74–75
Titus, Ebeneezer, 11
Tootsie's Orchid Lounge, 119–120, 121*
Torrance, Joe E., 116
Traveller's Rest, 108
Tulip Grove, 108
Tusculum, 9, 79
Two Rivers, 107–108

Union Hotel, 46–47
Union Station, 58*
University of Nashville, 18, 47,
    59–62, 124
Underwood, Doug, 103
Urban problems, 120–121

Vanderbilt, Cornelius, 59
Vanderbilt, William H., 59
Vanderbilt University, 59, 61, 62, 66–67,
    75–76, 77, 97, 100, 101, 110, 118, 121
Vauxhall Gardens, 26

WPA, 81, 86
Wade, John Donald, 77
Walden University, 50
Waldheim, Kurt, 109
Walker, Eliza, 49
Walker, Hugh, 125*
War of 1812, 16
War Memorial Building, 72, 88
Ward, William E., 97
Ward-Belmont College, 32, 97–99
Ward family, 10
Ward's Seminary, 97–98
Warfield, Charles, 116
Warren, Robert Penn, 76, 77
Watkins, J. F., 47
Watkins, Ron, 115
Watkins Institute, 57
Watkins, Samuel, 57, 105
Weather, 70, 82–83, 82*, 96
Wells, Heydon, 11

West, Ben, 97, 116
Western Military Institute, 59
Whigs, 25, 32–33, 34, 38, 50, 55, 56;
   campaign of 1844, 33
White, George, 48
White, Granny, 10
White, Zachariah, 10
Who Owns America?, 77
Wilhelm, Kaiser, 71
Williams, Albert S., 69
Williams, Avon T., 118
Williams, J. H., 47
Winchester, James, 108
Wills, Bob, 88
Wills, Ridley and Jesse, 76
Wilson, Joseph, 110

Wilson, Woodrow, 81, 109, 110
Winston family, 10
Woodmont Baptist Church, 120
Workhouse, 38
World War I, 70–72
World War II, 88–93
Wrencoe, 9

Young, R. A., 59
Young, Stark, 77

Zollicoffer, Felix Kirk, 27, 32–35, 39;
   views on secession, 34
Zolnay, George J., 78

About the Author

George Frank Burns is a graduate of Lebanon High School and Cumberland University. From 1943 to 1966 he was a reporter and editor of *The Lebanon Democrat,* and also wrote for *The Nashville Banner, The Tennessean,* and United Press International, contributing articles to *Time, Newsweek,* the *Christian Science Monitor* and *Billboard.*

In 1967, taking a Master of Arts from George Peabody College in English and history, he became public relations director and chairman of publications at Cumberland. In 1973 he earned a Ph.D. in English at Vanderbilt University. The following year he joined the faculty of Tennessee Technological University and retired in 1987.

Dr. Burns has studied at Oxford University, the University of London, and the Shakespeare Centre of the University of Birmingham, earning a certificate in genealogy and heraldry at Brasenose College, Oxford, in 1988. He is the author of the Tennessee County History Series volume on Wilson County and published a study of William Faulkner's Tennessee connections for Tennessee Homecoming '86. He has been commissioned to write a biography of Congressman Joe L. Evins and a history of Cumberland University.